BEDTIME STORIES FOR KIDS

Collection of short tales to help children fall asleep fast.

Fables for Kids, Animal Short Stories, Classic Fairy Tales, Princess Adventures and More.

Ages 2-6

Michelle Stone

Table of Contents

A Mouse in Jack's House

It has been almost a week since Jack noticed something unusual happening in his room. At night he could hear a strange sound, but he was unable to discover where the sound was coming from. Jack initially thought that it was just his imagination; however, Jack kept hearing the strange sound for about a week.

Other than the strange sound, Jack also found that whenever he put anything to eat on his table, that after a while half of the food was gone. Somebody was eating half of his food. Jack thought that it was his little brother.

One day Jack finally went to his little brother and asked him if he had been eating Jack's biscuits and berries from off of Jack's table. His little brother said that it has been more than a week since he went into Jack's room. Jack's mother also told him that no one goes into Jack's room even in his absence. Jack finally told his mother about the unusual things that he has been noticing for a couple of days. He told his mother about the strange sounds he hears every day. Jack further said to his mother that he felt as if it was a ghost. To this, his mother said that ghosts only exist in stories; they do not exist in real life. Jack said to his mother, "If that is the case, then who makes the strange sounds and who eats my biscuits and my berries?" His mother told him that it might be an insect that does that. She told him that the next day she will spray insect killer in the room which will kill all the insects, and that unusual thing will not happen any more in his room.

That night Jack went to sleep. He was happy that from the next day onwards he will be rid of the strange sound that disturbs him the whole night. The next morning Jacks mother came to wake him up. She asked jack to go out of the room and stay in her room while she sprays in Jacks room. Jack obeyed his mother and stayed in his mother's room the whole day.

At night, Jack went back to his room. He was very happy that he would sleep peacefully, because he had gotten rid of that irritating insect. Jack lied down on his bed, and he tried to sleep. But, to his surprise he heard that sound again. This time, the sound was even louder and more irritating. Jack was frightened this time. He called his mother so that she too could listen to the sound and identify where it was coming from.

His mother came and sat on his bed next to him. The two of them then waited for the sound. After about 5 minutes the sound came again. His mother tried to figure out where the sound was coming from. She drew the curtains to see if there was anything behind them, but she found nothing. Then she looked here and there in the room, but she was unable to trace where the sound was coming from. After a while, she dragged the side table away from its corner to see if there was something behind it. To her surprise, she saw that there was a small mouse.

She screamed out loud, and moved back. The moment she dragged the table, the mouse ran. And soon the mouse disappeared from their sight. The two of them were surprised to see all the biscuits and berries there with the mouse, which the mouse had been collecting for so many days. Jack finally was able to discover the thing that had been bugging him for so long.

Jack told his mother that the sound was really very irritating. He could not sleep the whole night because of it. His mother told him that they will soon figure out a way to catch the mouse. He asked his mother, "What are the possible ways through which we can catch the mouse?" His mother told him that she had a mouse trap, through which they can easily catch the mouse. She further said that they need to place some berries or anything else that mice like to eat near the trap, so that the mouse would see the food and come near the trap.

Jack asked his mother if it was necessary to kill the mouse. He wanted to take the mouse out of his room-- not to kill it. To this his mother said that they need to be a little careful. The moment the mouse is trapped, they immediately need to take the trap out and open it so that the mouse could escape safely.

Saying this, his mother went out of his room to get the trap and some berries. After a while, she was back with the items. She placed the trap near the side table, and on the trap she placed some almonds and berries. Jack and his mother sat on Jac bed without making any noise. His mother asked Jack to be silent, otherwise the mouse will not come out from its hiding place. They waited for the mouse to come close to the trap and get caught. Their eyes were on the trap.

After about half an hour, they could finally see the mouse approaching the trap. The mouse looked here and there. In the next moment, the mouse saw the berries and almonds and rushed to eat them. The moment the mouse got closer to the food and tried to eat it, the mouse was trapped.

Both Jack and his mother stood up immediately and went closer to the mouse. They dragged the trap with the help of a broom. Outside of their house, at the main gate, they opened the trap and helped the mouse to escape. Jack saw that the mouse was unable to run fast like before. He realized that one of its legs were hurt. He felt bad for the mouse. However, he was happy that he would finally be able to get sound sleep. From that day onwards, Jack slept peacefully.

LYNN'S BIRTHDAY PARTY

Lynn Morison was having her first birthday party ever, and she was so happy. She had her birthday planned in her mind, and she was so happy that her mother agreed to give a party for her.

That night, Lynn had turned all night dreaming, smiling and sleeping at the same time. She couldn't stop thinking about all the fun she was going to have with her friends at the party that was coming up, four days from that night when she was finally going to be seven.

The next day, Lynn woke up early and was about to walk into the kitchen to say hello to Mom and Grandma when she heard their conversation.

"There's not enough money to give her a big party, and I really want her to have fun and be happy with the party. That means I have to work hard for the next three days," her mother said sadly.

"Well, you don't have to give her a big party, for her to be happy, my dear," Grandma said. " All you have to do is stick to your budget and pray that things go well".

Lynn was sad that her mother had trouble getting ready for her birthday and even wanted to do something more for her. She thought of a way to cheer her up and make her smile when she finally had an idea.

On her way home from school, she had bought flowers for her mother with the money she was saving and when she came home, she saw her mother write a list of things to buy.

"Good afternoon, I bought you this," she said and gave her the flowers.

"Thank you dear, but I'm not the one celebrating," her mother said with a smile.

"I know, I heard you and Grandma talking about my birthday this morning. You don't have to give me a big party, Mom. The fact that you're giving me a party makes me happy and no matter how small it may be, it will make me happy"

Mrs. Morison had smiled and kissed her on the head.

"Thanks for understanding, honey".

"You're welcome, Mom," Lynn answered and went to her room.

Lynn came to school the next day and invited all her friends, plus her classmates. She wanted everyone to be there, and she was so anxious about her birthday.

At the breakfast table, on the morning of her birthday, she sat there with concern.

"What's wrong, Lynn, honey? Why the worried look on your face? You should be happy today".

"I'm so excited about my birthday, but I wonder if anyone will show up".

"Of course they will. I don't think your friends would want to miss your birthday. They should know how much it means to you," said Mrs. Morison, smiling and kissing her. " I think it should be full of color because it's you, my princess, who celebrates".

"So when are we going to the store to get my cake?"

"Soon darling, soon. Finish your breakfast first !"

Lynn and her mother went to the store. There she saw many sweets, the big ones, the small ones, tall ones and short ones, not to mention the ones with a strange aspect. Lynn finally picked out a cake she liked and one that was in the budget. The one in the budget was what her mother could afford, and she liked it, too.

On their way home, she kept thanking her mother for letting her have a party.

"Ha-ha, you've thanked me enough, honey".

"I don't think, you deserve more thanks".

"Ha-ha, anything for my princess," Mrs. Morison said with a smile.

Lynn had smiled and they laughed and sang together on their way home.

It was 5 p.m. and Mrs. Morison and her mother had already decorated the room, turning the whole room into something beautiful before the party. Then 5:30 p.m. arrived and by then Lynn had friends who arrived with lots of gifts, some large, some small and even long and short ones.

The room looked beautiful and colorful and some of his friends were already present, all dressed in colorful clothes. She had looked out of the window and saw some of her friends walking to her front door and it had given her so much joy.

It was finally time to make a wish and she expressed it before she blew out the candle on her cake. The rest of the evening had been filled with their voices as they laughed and danced for the songs that were played.

Even though her party wasn't as big as she had dreamed, Lynn and her friends had fun and that was all that mattered to her. That was really fun.

"Thanks, mom, thanks grandma. I had a great time and I can't wait to celebrate my birthday again," she said as they were giving each other a group hug.

Summary:

True happiness comes from within. You can have everything and still not be happy and you can have little and have all the joy of the world. So don't let what you have to affect your happiness because we all deserve to be happy in our own little way.

CHARLIE, THE BOY WHO HATED SCHOOL

Charlie was a five-year-old boy who hated school and everything about it. He hated reading, especially homework and projects, and his parents were worried. Every time his mother took him to school, he found a way to make trouble. For example, he pretended to be terribly ill so that his mother would be called from school to take him home. All Charlie liked to do was play and camp and nothing else. Charlie had a friend named Andy who lived across the street and came to Charlie's many times to play. Andy and Charlie were in the same class and they were best friends, but the difference between them was that Andy loved school and he never missed a day of school. Charlie hated school and all you saw him doing was playing instead of going to school.

When Andy played, he often sang the rhymes he learned in school. Charlie used to listen to Andy sing the rhymes but every time Andy offered to teach her Charlie frowned and told him he didn't care.

One day, when they were playing at Charlie's, Andy started singing one of his favorite rhymes:

Jack and Jill went up the hill

To fetch a pail of water
Jack fell down and broke his crown
And Jill came tumbling after

Jack got up and home did trot
As fast as he could caper
To old Dame Dob who patched his Nob
With vinegar and brown paper

Jack and Jill went up the hill
To fetch a pail of water
Jack fell and broke his crown
And Jill came tumbling after.

He noticed that Charlie nodded his head at the verses and again offered to teach him, but as usual Charlie refused him. Before Andy left Charlie's house, he reminded him of the next exam and reminded him that anyone who failed the exam couldn't join the next camp. As usual, Charlie laughed and told him they said it just to scare him into reading. With no luck convincing Charlie, Andy left with a sad face.

For days Andy didn't go to play, and that worried Charlie so much that he decided to go check it out. On his way to Andy's house, his mom opened the door and smiled at him when she saw Charlie standing in front of the door.

"Hi Charlie, how are you?" he asked.

"I'm fine, thank you, Mrs Stephens. Is Andy home?" Charlie asked.

"Yes," she replied.

"Can't he come to play only this time? I haven't seen him for a few days".

"Oh, I'm sorry, honey, but Andy's studying for the school exam and he'll come out when he's done with the exam. But I'll let him know you came looking for him," said Mrs Stephens, and gave Charlie a smile and watched him go down the porch. Charlie went home disappointed and went to his room to play alone.

The following week the exams began and after each exam Charlie waited for Andy to go home together. On the way home, Charlie was still doing his best to convince Andy to go play, but every time Andy refused. After the exams, Andy went to Charlie's house and played until the evening. Days later the results came out. Andy passed them, but Charlie didn't, but this didn't touch him at all. Charlie sat with Andy and his buddies so the bus would take them to the school camp. As soon as the bus came to the school stop, Mrs Stein came out of the bus with a list and started calling names. He called Andy but not Charlie. "Mrs Stein, I didn't hear my name," Charlie said confused by what was happening. " The camp is only for students who have passed the exam and clearly you did not pass it," she said folding the list.

"It,s not right, Danny and Ben can go too, and I can't?" "Yes, they can because they studied a lot to pass the exam and so they earned it," she answered. " I thought it was just a way to make us read and that what she said didn't matter".

"Well, actually, it was to get you to study, which you didn't take seriously from the look of it. Your score was very poor so I suggest you go home and study a lot for the next camp," she replied and returned to the bus before it left.

Charlie came home very angry and even when his mom tried to find out what was wrong, he refused to say a word. He locked himself in his room crying for days before deciding not to miss a camp and study.

When the school resumed, Charlie was always studying and that made his parents happy. From time to time, he even invited Andy to study and then play. Andy taught him some of the nursery rhymes he knew, and on their way home they sang them together on the bus. During the exam period Charlie excelled, and this time his name was on the list for the school camp and that made him happy. From then on he loved studying and excelled in many school activities.

Summary:
When you study you help yourself by increasing your knowledge and learning things. And besides, you better do things while others are doing them, so when the time comes for the reward, you won't be excluded, like Charlie, who learned the lesson and became better.

CRANK: THE ROBOT KID

Crank is a 6-year-old robot boy who had many superpowers, one of which allows him to change into an android plane. He lived in an oval world, as that place had been called, with his 3 human friends and a chicken; Naomi, Ariel, Akko and Nibbs. Ariel is a 7-year-old boy with great superpowers: he creates a force field with his hands and forms a shield. Akko is an 8-year-old boy, also with superpowers: he teleports. Naomi is a 6-year-old girl without powers. Nibbs is a chicken that is smart enough.

There was also an evil warlord who wanted to destroy the oval world because of how happy they lived together and his name was Drago. He wanted to catch Nibbs because he needed him to build a huge bomb for him.

One Saturday morning, Nibbs wanted to go see Crank because he needed some clarification on a project he was working on. Nibbs was smart, but he knew the crank was much smarter. Nibbs came to a crossroads; he felt that something was wrong because the whole place was awfully quiet. Suddenly he felt something on his neck.

"What is it?" she thought out loud holding a needle.

A few seconds after his vision began to blur and some monkeys began to approach him, he knew they were from Drago, but he could do nothing because he had become too weak.

It was Sunday and crank and his friends have not yet seen Nibbs. He had never been the type to leave without leaving a message.

"Are you sure you checked his house?" Crank asked Ariel.

"Yes, I did, I even asked her neighbors where she was," said Ariel.

"Where can he be then?" Crank asked worriedly.

"Why don't we go ask around?" Naomi asked as she stood up from where she was sitting.

They headed to the streets in search of Nibbs. Crank saw an old man who was struggling to transport his goods and he approached him.

"Where are you going?" Ariel asked.

"That old man needs help", Crank replied.

"Well, you know we're still looking for Nibbs, right?" Ariel asked again.

"Looking for Nibbs doesn't mean we shouldn't help someone who needs help", replied Crank, walking towards the man.

Everyone decided to work together to help the old man, for his goods were many.

"Hello sir, can I help you?", Crank offered.

"Ah yes, my old back gave up" the old man said laughing.

Crank asked Akko to tie the goods with a rope that was on the floor and teleport them into his cargo, as he turned into an android plane. Akko did exactly what Crank asked him and then came back to teleport his other friends and the old man on the plane.

At the old man's house, they helped him sort out his stuff in his warehouse.

"The person you're looking for has been taken away by some monkeys," said the old man, swinging his chair.

"Seriously, how did you know that we were looking for someone?", Crank asked, surprised.

"Your friend tried to remind you of what you should have done," he said, swinging his chair again. " It's better to go save him first and come back for answers later," he added.

"Thank you very much sir," crank said, without wasting any time asking any more questions. So they left the old man's house.

They walked for a while and realized they wouldn't get far on foot.

"Those monkeys belong to Drago, right?" Akko asked.

"Yes, and I wonder why they took Nibbs," Crank said.

Crank turned into his android plane and the others entered. He flew beyond the oval world and entered the forest that was home to Drago. Crank used his infrared vision to locate the house and saw Nibbs chained to a pole.

"I've located Nibbs," said Crank from the control panel speakers.

"Okay, how do we get him out?" Naomi asked.

"Akko, you can teleport in and out of there, while Ariel, you can protect me with your shield, because we could be attacked".

Crank landed on forest land, Ariel installed the shield, while Akko teleported. The monkeys ran towards them, laying their guns and shooting at the plane, but the bullets kept bouncing. Crank dropped a bomb that exploded in front of the monkeys, and they dispersed.

Akko went out a few minutes later with Nibbs in his hand and teleported on the plane and they left.

"Are you all right Nibbs?" Naomi asked

"Yes, I just need food," said Nibbs as his legs shook visibly.

They all laughed and went back to the old man's house.

"How did you know who we were looking for and who took it?" Crank asked the old man.

"Well, an old man knows everything, and I saw the monkey leave the kingdom with him," said the old man.

"But how did you know we were looking for a chicken?" Akko asked.

"You guys are very popular around here, and since the monkeys who kidnapped him were from Drago, I knew it would be one of you guys coming," added the old man.

"And why did you help us? You barely know us!" Akko asked again.

"Ah-ah, you didn't even know me and you helped me, you also showed me respect, which most people don't and I think one favor deserves another in return," said the old man smiling.

"Well, thank you so much for your help, now, with your permission," Crank said, getting up from the chair he was sitting in.

"Now you see the value of respect and helping people, right?" Crank told his friends that initially they didn't want to help.

"Yes," they all answered.

Summary:

When you help someone who needs, you feel good about yourself and you also bring a smile on the other person's face. Try to help someone today, because you never know what that person could do for you and, whoever he is, he could come back to help you one day. Remember, a good turn deserves another.

AVA THE GREAT

Ava-Grace is a chubby six-year-old girl with big brown eyes. She has a sparkling personality and always wears a bright smile. She loves swimming; playing outdoors with her friends, dancing and playing in the park, especially with the swings because she thinks they make her fly like a superhero. Ava dreams of becoming a superhero to help people like her mother, who's a nurse. She wants to help spread the love around the world because she loves seeing happy people. She hates being in the dark, clowns, and even insects.

Ava-Grace lives with her mother, her grandmother Mary and her adoring and protective uncles Andre, Larry and Richard. She never met her father, and she never asked her mother, because her grandmother said she should talk to her mother when she was old enough. She spends most of her time alone with her grandmother because the three uncles work far away in Texas, and her mother comes home late. Most of the time she was already in bed before her mother came home, and the only time she can be with her mother is mostly on Fridays and Sundays. But that never stopped her from being worshipped, cuddled and treated like a princess because she was the only daughter and granddaughter Grandma Mary had. Ava-Grace likes to call her grandmother Nana often, even though she doesn't know how the name was born, but grandma loved being called that.

Ava-Grace's mom was in the kitchen making dinner while Ava Grace was in the living room practicing her dance moves for the approaching school pageant.

"Ava, please prepare the dining table, dinner is almost ready," his mother called from the kitchen.

"Okay, mom" Ava answered turning off the music and going into the dining room. Her mother had baked her favorite food that was apple pie and that made her very happy.

After dinner, her mother took Ava to her room to prepare her for bed because it was almost time for bed. Her mother sat next to her while she lay on the bed before kissing her forehead.

"Good night," she said and was about to leave when Ava-Grace asked:

"Are you coming to the pageant, Mom?"

"Of course, dear, I would never miss it for anything in the world. You come first," she answered with a smile and kissed her again on the forehead. " Now go to bed," she said and she had left the room.

On the day of the pageant, Ava-Grace went to school early, with her mother and her grandmother, and together they had cheered for her. She only came out of the pageant with the second place.

"You danced well, dear, you didn't know you had those moves in you. I have to say that you danced very much like me when I was your age. But I was better!" said Grandma and they laughed on the way home.

When they got home, Ava's mother got a phone call and had to leave. Ava-Grace and her grandmother had sat down together to watch a movie, Ava had gone to the kitchen to get water and when she had come back she had seen her grandmother lying on the floor. She had rushed to her side and noticed that she was not breathing well. Quickly, she picked up his phone and called 911 before calling his mother. Soon an ambulance arrived and took his grandmother to the hospital.

"Mom," Ava called with a worried look as her mother came to tuck her in.

"Yes, honey, what's wrong, dear? You look worried," she added as she sat on her bed.

"Is Grandma gonna be okay?"

"She certainly will be, dear".

"I wish I had superpowers so I could be a superhero

and save Nana and help people around me," Ava had said in a sad tone.

"Oh dear, you don't need to have a superpower to be a superhero," her mother said. " You know, you saved Nana's life today, and in my books, that makes you a super hero".

"Really?" Ava said with a surprised look.

"Of course, my darling," her mother replied. " You don't necessarily have to wear a cape to see yourself as a hero. What makes you a hero is inside you. Just like what you did for Nana today, that makes you a real hero".

"Wow mom! I'm a superhero after all", she said excitedly, and they both laughed.

"Yes, my darling, you certainly are," said her mother.

"Good night, Mom," Ava said smiling.

"Good night and sweet dreams dear," her mother replied.

Ava was lying in bed with what her mother had just told going through her mind.

"So I'm finally a hero, now I can be whatever I choose to be," she thought out loud.

She had thought for a while before falling asleep. She had found herself in a dream country where she helped other children in danger. She was wearing a blue superhero cape with the words "AVA THE GREAT" written boldly on her chest. She saved the children from the bullies at school, always in the right place and even on time. The bullies were afraid of her and they never had to show up again. There is love, peace and kindness in school, all thanks to AVA THE GREAT. All the children loved her and often shouted her name "AVA THE GREAT!"

BEN AND HARPER

Once upon a time there was a cat named Harper. Harper was brown, with curly hair and charming blue eyes. She lived in a big house with her owner Mrs. Martha who was very fond of her. Mrs. Martha took Harper everywhere she went. Mrs. Martha even got her a personalized gold tag, which she always wore around her neck. All the other cats were jealous of Harper because she was unique.

One Saturday morning, Harper and Mrs. Martha went to the mall to get groceries. On the way back, Mrs. Martha remembered she forgot to get cat food.

"Oh no, I forgot to get your food at the mall," said Mrs. Martha. "You stay here, let me go quickly to get your food," she added.

"All right," Harper replied.

Mrs. Martha quickly went to get cat food at the mall. Harper was standing on the side of the road waiting for his owner to come back.

Suddenly, she heard a loud noise behind a big tree. She got closer to check what was going on. At that moment, a big wild dog came out of a hole under a big tree.

"I'll eat you!" exclaimed the wild dog in a terrifying voice.

Harper immediately started running to save his life, with the big wild dog chasing her furiously.

"Do you think you can outrun me?" said the wild dog.

"I'm twice as fast as you," added the wild dog.

Harper knew she couldn't outrun the wild dog, so she started zigzagging and eventually beat the big wild dog. She immediately hid in a drainage pipe and waited for the big wild dog to leave. The wild dog searched for Harper for a few minutes and eventually left.

"Thank God, that was close," Harper said.

"It's time to go home, Mrs. Martha should have gone home by now," she added.

Harper came out of her hiding place and started going home.

"Oh no, this place looks weird," she said, "I think I'm lost".

She laid down under a small tree and began to cry having lost all hope. Afraid and hungry, she noticed a shadow walking towards her. She got up quickly and tried to escape.

"Don't be afraid, I'm not here to hurt you".

"My name is Ben, what's your name?" the shadow asked approaching and it turned out to be another dog.

"I'm Harper," she said dodging scared.

"I know you're scared, because I'm a dog. I promise I'm not here to attack you, but to help you. Tell me, what's wrong? Why are you crying?" Ben asked while he was sitting next to Harper.

"I can't find my way home," Harper replied with a low tone.

"That is so sad!"

"How did you get lost?" Ben asked.

Harper told her story in tears. Ben took pity on Harper and offered to take her home.

"Don't worry, Harper, I'll take you to my house. I live with my master George, a few blocks down the street" Ben had said indicating a dark red and yellow house down the street.

"I'm not sure this is a good idea," Harper said.

"Why?" Ben asked.

"I don't think your master George will be happy with that. And besides, dogs and cats don't get along," Harper replied.

"Don't worry, George is the nicest person I know, he found me trapped, just like I found you," Ben said.

"Look at me and look at you, what differences do you see?" Ben asked.

"None," Harper replied.

"So you see, you're not different from me," Ben said.

"We are one," he added.

"Yes, it's true," Harper replied with a smile.

"Let's go home," Ben said.

Harper followed Ben and they chatted as they walked to Ben's house. By the time they got home, Ben's owner had not yet returned. Ben knew Harper was hungry, so he went into the kitchen, took the food his master left for him and gave it to him.

"Here, take these, I know you're starving," Ben said.

"Thank you, Ben," Harper replied.

A few minutes later, George came in and saw how the cat and the dog got along. He couldn't believe what he had seen.

"Looks like you made a new friend, Ben," said George staring at them.

"What's your name?" George asked while he was checking the tag around her neck.

"Harper."

"You look lost, Harper."

"Your master will be worried about you," George added as he lifted it and caressed her fur. Harper had told her story to George, and also how Ben had helped her. He felt pity and compassion for Harper.

"Ben, I'm proud of you," said George.

"Master, you did the same when you found me homeless and wandering the street," Ben replied.

"Oh yes, one good deed deserves another in return," said George while caressing Ben on the head.

"I'm a little surprised at how you got along with Harper," he added.

"I see no difference between us," Ben replied.

"We are one," he added.

"Oh yes, it's a valuable lesson," said George.

"We are a big family" he added with a smile.

They all laughed with joy.

"So Harper, what's your master's name?" George asked.

"Mrs. Martha" replied.

"Oh I know her, her house is only a few miles away," said George.

"Can you take me there?" Harper asked.

"Yes, of course, but not before you take a shower," George replied.

Later that night, George, Harper and Ben arrived at Mrs. Martha's house. She was happy and grateful to have found her cat, all thanks to Ben.

From that day on, Ben and Harper visited each other. They shared everything together and also played together. They became best friends despite their differences.

Summary:
Despite what people say about cats and dogs, Harper and Ben did not see any difference between them, but they believed to be one. So we should love each other, no matter what our differences are.

THE BEAUTY CROWN OF ARYA

Alma and Kareem had a beautiful daughter named Arya. Arya had curly dark hair and a beautiful smile that everyone admired. She was very smart and was good at school. Arya was the only daughter of her parents and so she was very special to them and had brought joy into their lives.

Arya grew up being very beautiful, very smart and tall. When she was six, her parents had bought her a ticket to the Miss Sunshine pageant for her exceptional beauty and charm.

The night before pageant day, she was completely awake and walking around her room.

She was so nervous, she didn't notice her mother coming in.

"Nervous?" her mother asked.

She turned and saw her mother standing at her door and ran towards her to hug her.

"I don't know if I can do this, Mom," she said, holding her and crying.

"You know what I think?" her mother said, leaning over to her face before wiping her tears with a handkerchief.

"No, mom".

"I think you're the smartest girl I know, and smart girls never get discouraged. Rather they build their strength through their weakness. I know you can, my angel".

"Do you think so, mom?" she asked.

"No, I don't think so, I know it. Now go to bed, you have a big day tomorrow and a crown to win," her mother answered smiling as Arya climbed on her bed.

"Thanks mom and good night," said Arya while her mother was closing the door.

"Good night, honey, sleep well," she said and she closed the door.

Arya sat quietly in the car while her parents took her to the Miss Sunshine pageant the next morning. She was still a little nervous and tried to calm down by looking out the car window to distract herself.

"Everything will be fine, honey," said his mother. "Everything will be fine".

"Your mother is right, everything will be fine" his father added. "Go and have fun, you can do it".

"Thanks mom, thanks dad," Arya answered.

And so the contest had begun and it was more or less a tight contest, as every girl wanted to win.

Arya was in the top three of Miss Sunshine pageant. She was on stage holding hands with the other girls waiting for the winner to be announced. She was scared and nervous at the same time. She was afraid she might not win, and she was nervous to be called the winner. Her hands were sweaty, but she remembered what her parents had told her before and so she regained confidence.

"The winner of the Miss Sunshine contest is…. Stacy!" exclaimed the woman with the microphone.

Arya had almost burst into tears but had held her head up and smiled. Even though Arya didn't win, she gave Stacy a hug and congratulated her on her victory.

"You did well, honey!" her father said.

"I tried my best, Dad", she said crying.

"Don't worry, honey," said her mother, holding her in her arms.

"You did well, for us you are the winner and we are proud of you," she added.

"But I didn't win, Mom!"

"There is always a next time dear. You will surely win the next one. Don't let this break your confidence," added her father.

A month after Miss Sunshine pageant, Arya's mother came home with a form. She wanted to surprise her daughter.

"Arya, come downstairs, I have something for you," her mother called Arya, who was upstairs in her room.

"Okay mom," said Arya as she ran to the living room. She had seen her mom sitting on the couch smiling at her.

"How are you today?" her mom asked .

"Well, mom," Arya answered, wondering why she was still smiling.

"I have something for you here," said her mother when she gave her the form she came home with.

"This is a form for Little Miss Congeniality contest !" said Arya surprised.

"Yes, and the organizers want you to participate".

"I'm happy about this, but I can't. And if I lose again, Mom?" Arya asked.

"We don't know yet", her mother answered. "Let's give it a try".

"I don't know, Mom. But do you think I'll have a chance?"

"Definitely my dear. You came close to winning the first contest, so I think you have every chance of winning this one," she said stroking his hair.

"Okay, mom, thank you," Arya said, and she hugged her.

Three weeks later, the event had begun and Arya was full of confidence. She was very positive about this event and decided that the result didn't matter : she wouldn't let it affect her. At that moment, she saw Stacy among the contestants, but she wasn't bothered. The room was full of people coming to show support for the contestants of the Little Miss Congeniality contest. Arya had passed the first levels and in the last three she was again with Stacy in the last three. The three girls were silent as they waited for the winner to be announced.

"And now, the moment we've all been waiting for, the winner of this year's competition is... Arya!" exclaimed the anchor of the show.

Arya for a moment had not understood what had just happened, she looked at her parents and saw them clapping and only after she realized that she had won, when Stacy walked towards her and said:

"You deserve it, congratulations".

The excitement and shock passed and even after the host had put the crown on her head, she still could not believe she had won.

"Mom, I made it," said Arya while her mother went up on stage to meet her.

"Yes, honey, we did it," said his mother while they were both laughing.

BEAUTIFUL BERYLA

Once upon a time there was a beautiful kingdom called Beryla. There were so many colorful flowers and fruit trees in every house in the kingdom. The streets were made of shining gold. There were many wild animals, but they did not harm anyone: there were tigers, dragons, dinosaurs, lions, chimpanzees and many others. At night, thousands of fireflies adorned the night making the kingdom shine. Everyone was happy and did everything together. The kingdom was peaceful.

Something tragic happened one day and changed everything in the kingdom. The king and queen were killed by an evil witch named Avalon, leaving their only daughter, Princess Lucy alone and sad. The kingdom was powerless because the witch and her evil dragon held her hostage. No one had left the kingdom and no one had entered. From that day, the trees and flowers began to die, the fireflies stopped flying and the gold stopped shining. Everywhere it was dark.

Avalon took command of the kingdom and soon the kingdom began to lose its beauty, but not all, because the people still believed in the princess. Avalon, the witch, wanted the people to follow her by any means possible, to have the full power to rule the kingdom, but she discovered that their loyalty was to the princess and her family. This made her red with rage and so she decided to kill the princess, because she was the only one standing between her and her evil plan.

Meanwhile, Princess Lucy was always crying and every time she cried, it rained a lot. She missed her parents very much. She wished they were still alive. Everyone tried to stop Avalon, but they could not, and soon it was clear that they would surrender.

One day, a very old mouse named Tita, who was a loyal servant of her father, came to see her secretly. He always sneaked into the royal castle and then into the room where Princess Lucy was closed by a small hole.

"Princess, why are you still crying for your parents? This is not the time to cry because Avalon the witch is trying to win the hearts of the people and when she does, there will be nothing left to rule in the kingdom".

"But why should I be happy when my mom and dad died? Look at our beloved kingdom that once had the glory and lost everything, looks what it has become now" Lucy replied. " Even if I were allowed to escape, how can I fight her?" she said crying. And every time she cried, it rained heavily in the kingdom. Then he ran away to his house before the streets were flooded.

When the rat came down to the castle the next day and again met the princess Lucy, she was in the same condition as the previous day and he said again:

"Princess Lucy, do you know why the people refused to follow Avalon? It's because of you, Princess Lucy. They depend on you and only you to help them. So trust me and stop crying and be happy. Just sing to change".

Every time the princess wanted to try to sing, she ended up crying again.

Then one day Avalon came to meet Lucy in her room and took her out, where people had gathered, into the courtyard of the palace. She was tired of people refusing to follow her because of the princess. She took her out with the force and ordered her evil dragon to eat her in front of her people. Perhaps, when they see that she is dead, they will be forced to follow him. Lucy was afraid and had started to cry. In the meantime Tita had made his way towards the front of the crowd and then shouted: "Lucy, stop crying, be happy and sing the song that your mother used to sing to you. You just need to trust me on this one".

Lucy knew it was the same rat who was sneaking into her room. Lucy was too scared to do anything, but since she was going to die anyway, there was nothing wrong with trying what the old rat asked her to do, she thought before she decided to sing. She sang the same song her mother sang to her. She sang and sang until she started dancing and everyone else joined her in the song, and they danced and sang with joy. Soon the trees and flowers had blossomed and they too had begun to dance. The streets began to shine again. They shone so brightly that their splendor pursued Avalon and her dragon, so that they fled far from the castle to be seen no more.

After that day, everything returned to normal. The Kingdom was beautiful again. But Lucy and everyone wondered why their song brought everything back to life. Tita the rat had told them: "Every time Princess Lucy cries, it rains, when she is sad, everywhere is wet, when she is afraid everything else vanishes. We're all connected and everything you do affects everything, including humans. Your mother was once a goddess and passed her power to you, which is to give life, but you never knew, only your father and I knew it," Tita said.

From that day on, Princess Lucy reigned as the Supreme Princess and guarded every creature that lived in her kingdom and finally there was peace throughout the kingdom.

Summary:

Encouragement, sometimes, is all we need to take that extra step and bring out the greatness, the best of ourselves and others. We should not learn to give up easily but learn to encourage ourselves and stay strong. Try to encourage someone today.

AS RABBIT AND TIME BECAME FRIENDS

Rabbit laid on his bed, tired from all the things he had done that afternoon. He didn't have the energy to study or to help grandma with some of the chores.

She got out of bed and went to get the book. She tried to study and do her homework but was too tired to do it.

"I'll only sleep for a minute," said Rabbit to herself as she went to bed and fell asleep. Waking up from his nap, which she needed, she looked at the time, hoping to continue her studies. "Six o'clock in the morning!", she screamed, and ran out of the room running to the living room so she could talk to grandma.

"I'm sorry I couldn't help you yesterday, Grandma," said Rabbit after meeting Grandma in the living room.

"Good morning to you too"; said the grandmother. " Why are you running?"

"Sorry, good morning grandma"; said Rabbit."I am so sorry for yesterday, I was so tired from playing that I decided to sleep for a few minutes, but when I woke up it was morning".

"Well, you didn't spend your time well," said Grandma. "Don't worry. Go take a bath and get ready for school".

"Aren't you mad at me?" Rabbit asked.

"Of course not, dear," said Grandma. "Your lunchbox is on the table with your breakfast. Your mom wanted me to make sure that you would eat before school. She had to go to work very early today," she added.

"Okay, Grandma," said Rabbit on her way to get ready for school.

"I can't handle my time," she whispered to herself.

The day of Rabbit at school did not go very well because many of his teachers were angry because she had not done her homework and did not take the studies seriously.

Feeling the need to be alone, Rabbit, after school, sat in the playground.

"Why are you alone?" asked Pigeon, a friend of hers.

"I'm trying to understand why it's hard for me to do things like study and help my grandmother while it's easy to do fun things like play"; answered Rabbit.

"Well, I think you're overthinking it," said Pigeon, trying to cheer up his friend.

"Do you think that?" Rabbit asked.

"Yes," said Pigeon. "Come on, let's go play. I know this will cheer you up".

They went together to Rabbit's house, where they played for two hours.

"Thank you for cheering me up," said Rabbit to Pigeon.

"You're welcome", said Pigeon. "I'm going. Make sure you do your homework today".

"I will," replied Rabbit.

After her friend had left, Rabbit took the book to study and do his homework, but ended up falling asleep while she was studying.

"Good morning, Mom," Rabbit greeted his mother while she was in the kitchen making breakfast.

"Good morning dear," said Mrs. Rabbit. "I hope you slept well," she added.

"Yes, mom," sadly said Rabbit.

"What's wrong, dear, are you all right?" Mrs. Rabbit asked after noticing how sad Rabbit was.

"Mom, I don't know how to handle my time. These days I always end up not studying or doing my homework, I don't have time to tidy up my room or to help grandma with some of the housework," Rabbit said crying.

"Oh dear," said Mrs. Rabbit while she was drying her tears. "It's not your fault, time flies".

"Does time fly?" Rabbit asked, not knowing what it meant.

"Yes dear, time flies".

After hearing his mother say that time was flying, Rabbit was determined to take his time and put it in a cage. She was thinking about forcing time to be with her while she did whatever she wanted.

"Rabbit, I want to see you after class," said her teacher. He was her favorite teacher, and it frightened her that he wanted to see her right away. She wondered what she'd done wrong this time.

"He wanted to see me, sir," Rabbit asked when he arrived in his office.

"Yes, come in and sit down," said the teacher.

"Thank you, sir,"

Rabbit sat in a chair in front of her teacher.

"I'm not happy with your studies," said the teacher. " You haven't done your homework lately, what's going on?"

"I'm sorry, sir, it's because time flies a lot and I barely have time to do things. But don't worry, I have a plan to take the time and get him by my side".

"Oh dear, you can't capture time," said the teacher.

"Can't I? But my mother said time flies, so doesn't that mean I can take it?"

"This is not what he meant", explained the teacher. "All he meant was that you have to use your time well".

"How can I do that?" Rabbit asked.

"Well, you can talk to Ant," said the teacher, "She knows how to use and make friends with her time. You know her, she's in your class."

"Thank you very much, sir," said Rabbit as she left the office.

After school that day, Rabbit went to Ant to ask her about the time.

"Hi, can I talk to you, please?" Rabbit asked.

"Yes, what is it?" replied Ant.

"Can you tell me your secret about how you became friends with time?" said Rabbit. "I also want to be friends with time".

"It's easy," replied Ant. "I make sure to do all the non-fun things, like tidying up my room, reading my books and doing my chores after school, before doing fun things like playing later in the evening. This way I do everything I have to do before the end of the day," she added.

"Wow, that's why time wasn't my friend, because I do funny things before," said Rabbit.

"Time has always been your friend, you just needed to use it well," replied Ant.

"Thank you so much for sharing," Rabbit said as she hugged Ant.

From that day on, Rabbit and time became best friends because she listened to the advice and managed her time well.

Summary:

There is time for everything, you just need to know how to split the time and make good use of it. How you use the time counts a lot.

FIZZY THE DINOSAUR

Once upon a time there was a dinosaur called Fizzy who loved to go out on adventures. He lived in the back of the village and had no friends or family, he was always alone. Fizzy was a curious and brave dinosaur who liked to play with butterflies and fireflies and also loved to look for new things and began every day willing to explore any new area he could find. His curiosity often brought him to unknown places and most of the time he camped outdoors because he loved nature, but he was always careful and always took precautions when camping outdoors. Fizzy started out with the same routine every day. He woke up as the sun rose, quickly found something to eat before going out on the street to explore and meet new people. Fizzy sometimes felt lonely and always hoped to make new friends on the street.

One day, there was an announcement: the princess had been kidnapped on her way to the Grand Ball in the next village, and the king had promised whoever found her a nice reward. Everyone was out looking, but Fizzy wasn't worried because he had other places to explore in his head.

So one-day Fizzy left his home for his usual adventure and this time he went a little beyond normal. On his way back, in the cold night, he noticed a big dinosaur moving strangely through the forest. He wanted to mind his own business, but his curiosity wouldn't let him, so he followed the dinosaur until he reached a hidden cave covered in bushes. He was not sure what was going on and had changed his mind about following the dinosaur into the cave, but he was forced after seeing the suspicious look on the dinosaur's face before he entered the cave. Fizzy wasn't a fan of the caves, but something in his gut told him something was wrong and so he entered the cave. He walked along the cave for a while and was about to surrender when he heard voices and so he walked slowly towards the voices and soon saw a light coming out of a part of the cave. " Please! I want to go home!" he heard a woman scream. "Stop begging, princess! You'll never get out of here" exclaimed the huge dinosaur laughing, and his two friends joined him. Fizzy approached to take a look and saw the young princess sitting on the floor and tied to a pole and also noticed that the three dinosaurs were dressed in the way the king's army was dressed.

"Oh, what should I do, how can I save her now?" he thought to himself.

He really wanted to help her, but Fizzy knew he wasn't a strong enough opponent for the three big dinosaurs and had no chance of winning in any physical combat. So he thought of the quickest way to do something. Immediately afterwards he came up with an idea. A little later he saw a small section where they had packed their food supplies. So he took out his camping lamp and set fire to the food supply. The dinosaurs did not notice the fire in time until one of them came to do his turn off control of the cave and cried to the others when he saw the fire. Fizzy was already waiting and praying that everyone left the room, and as soon as the princess was alone in the room, Fizzy quickly ran into the room, untied her and led her quickly out of the cave. He quickly set fire to the bushes at the entrance of the cave before escaping with the princess to their village.

As soon as he arrived at their village, he told the king what had happened, and immediately the king sent his army to the cave, and soon the three dinosaurs were captured.

"You really saved my life today and you were really brave".

"I just followed my instincts," Fizzy said as he watched the army drag the dinosaurs away.

The king was very happy to see his daughter safe. He hugged her very strongly and could not stop laughing. The next day a large party was held at which everyone in the village was invited. There the king gave his daughter to Fizzy as a wife and made him responsible for the safety of all the village. From that day on, the story of his life changed: from a dinosaur who lived at the end of the village without friends and family, to a dinosaur who had married a princess and had all the friends he could wish for.

And so Fizzy and the princess got married and lived happily ever after.

Summary:

Being curious sometimes helps, but not always. And remember that not all the situations in which you find yourself can be resolved by the struggle. Sometimes we need to be smart and use our brain. And as it helped fizzily, it could also help us.

PEA

It was a sunny day, the weather was beautiful and Pea today wanted to play, but he could not do it alone. So he had left his can (?) and had gone to Birdie's house thinking of going to visit Mash after. Birdie knocked on Birdie's door and soon Birdie opened the door.

"Hello Pea," Birdie said. "Isn't it a good day to go to play?"

"Yeah, I thought so, too, but I was thinking about going to see Mash see if he'd like to play with us".

"This is a great idea, but let me finish this cupcake before we leave," Birdie said and had hurried to finish his breakfast.

They ran together on the hill to visit Mash, and as they ran they began to sing;

The day is very bright
It's clear and it's sunny
The day is very bright
Enough to go out and play.

They met Mash a few miles from his house, he had his picnic basket with him.

"Where are you going to Mash?", Birdie asked.

"I was going to come to you and then later to Pea. I was coming to invite you two for a picnic".

"Ooh I'd love to! So I think we should find a suitable place for the picnic then," suggested Pea.

"How about if we do it on the field where you can (?) is, Pea ?" Birdie had suggested.

"I was thinking about it too. It would be perfect for our picnic," added Mash.

"Well, then. If you gentlemen want to follow me, then I will lead you to the camp," Pea said and he had made his way.

They had arrived at the camp and prepared the picnic table, sat down and enjoyed the view.

"Wow, the view from here is beautiful. No wonder that Pea barely comes out," Mash said eating a sandwich.

"Well, I would say that it is only a fortune if I have this view!", Pea had answered.

A few minutes later, they saw Mouse running towards them. It looked like something was chasing her and she was running really fast.

"What's wrong with Mouse?" Birdie asked.

"I saw the sky fall, just over the hedge".

Immediately, Mash and Birdie ran as fast as they could into Pea's can, leaving Pea that was already sleeping behind. Pea woke up a few minutes later and was surprised not to have found Mash and Birdie.

"Where could they have gone?" he thought out loud. " Well, I guess I'll have to go find them then," he added, and immediately went looking for his friends.

He had been thinking about the path his friends could take. He first came at Mash's, but he wasn't home, and then at Birdie's, who was not home too. "Where could they have gone?", he had asked, and had continued his research still reflecting. He soon came upon a turtle resting under an apple tree as apples fell from the tree. As he approached him and asked if he had seen his friends, an apple had fallen on the turtle, who suddenly woke up and started eating the apple.

"Good morning, Mr. Tortoise," Pea greeted.

"Hello, Pea".

"Doesn't the apple that falls on you bother you at all?" he asked.

"No, Pea, in fact I like to hear the sound they make when they hit the ground".

"And the tree, can it fall?"

"Yes, of course, and that's what might worry me, I should look for another place to rest," said Mr. Tortoise, eating another apple.

"Hmm, do you think the sky might fall one day?"

"I don't think so. I've been alive for years and I've seen trees fall, buildings fall, planes and a lot of other things fall, but never the sky. So I assure you that if you are standing under the sky, you are very safe".

"Have you seen Mash and Birdie?"

"No, I thought I saw you pass earlier," said Mr. Tortoise.

"Yes, but I woke up and didn't see them again".

"Okay, good luck finding them then," said Mr. Tortoise and he had returned to his rest, while Pea had continued the search for his friends.

"Where could they be?" he asked out loud as he walked.

"Right here, Pea, can you help us? We're stuck in here".

"How did you get stuck in my can?" asked Pea trying to get Birdie out.

"Mouse said that the sky was falling and so we decided to shelter here," said Mash after Pea had managed to pull them out.

"No Mash, the sky cannot fall from where it hangs. Mr. Tortoise told me so and, by the way, let's ask Mouse where he got that information," Pea said and they had gone looking for Mouse. They found him in the field where they were having their picnic eating their food.

"What are you doing?" Mash asked.

"I'm eating, sure," he replied.

"You deceived us by telling us that the sky was falling into pieces".

"Well, I must have said it out of hunger. Is there anything a hungry mouse wouldn't say?" he asked.

Pea and his friends had laughed while Mouse continued to eat until he had eaten his fill.

Summary:

Be careful what kind of information you share. People react differently to information, and as far as we are concerned, we should be sure of the source of our information before we react.

THE DRAGON EMPEROR

A long time ago, in a distant kingdom, lived a mystical and very powerful Dragon that created problems for everyone, leaving everyone frightened. The emperor wanted peace, but he didn't know how to convince the dragon.

Meanwhile, there was a boy named Wang, who lived in the forest outside the kingdom. He was a hunter who always went into the forest to hunt and sometimes he said he owned the forest not knowing he was sharing the forest with a powerful dragon.

One day, while he was hunting, he came across an egg deep in the forest, but he was not sure which animal had laid the egg and so he brought it home and kept it on a shelf.

One day the king fell seriously ill and it was said that he would not survive the disease. He had no son, only a daughter who had no right to rule, and so he was without an heir. And so he issued a decree that whoever killed or made the dragon go away would be given the throne and his daughter. So the words were spread throughout the kingdom, but they never reached Wang because he did not live near the kingdom.

Meanwhile Wang was always busy with his hunting and egg controlling, to know if it would hatch. But it was like it was taking forever to hatch, and so he would go do his usual business. He hunted and sold for profit until one day he came upon a young man in the forest who seemed lost and confused.

"Hello sir", Wang greeted him.

"Oh, thank goodness, finally someone" he had sighed in relief. "I think I lost my way home".

"Okay, where exactly are you coming from? Where are you going?"

"Well, I'm going back to the kingdom. I can't find my way through a forest, let alone fight a dragon. All for a princess," the man said.

"A dragon, here in the forest?" Wang asked surprised, hearing it for the first time.

"You look surprised. Do you hear it for the first time?"

"Yes, sir, but no wonder. People rarely enter the forest to hunt as before," he replied.

"Well, you should know that, too. The king has issued a decree that whoever kills or sends away the dragon will inherit his kingdom and marry his daughter," said the man.

"I'm not interested in the kingdom, sir, but you should want to go home. Take the first right from here and then there is a straight path.

"Thank you," said the man.

"The pleasure is mine," said Wang who was still thinking about what the man had just said about a dragon living in his own forest.

Soon, other strangers began to enter and exit the forest. Wang could do nothing but wait because he didn't want to be eaten by the dragon.

Many people had entered the cave and never returned, and so, in the end, he decided to go and see what the dragon looked like. He got ready and decided to go the next day.

And so Wang began his journey to the hill with a bow and arrow and took with him the egg he had found in the forest. He kept walking until he arrived at the opening of a cave.

"This must be it," he said and began to walk to the entrance.

As he entered the cave, he was not sure what he was going to see or what he expected to see, but one thing was certain in his mind and it was his plan to see the dragon. When he entered the cave, suddenly there were two eyes staring at him.

"What brings you to my cave, human?" asked the dragon with a deep voice.

"I just came to see you, but now I also want to ask you a favor".

"What? How dare you come into my cave and ask me a favor? I could eat you right now".

"I know you're more powerful and stronger than I am, but I want to beg you, can you please leave us alone and stop scaring us?"

"No, not at all. I lost someone special to me, my egg. And your king took it" replied the dragon.

At that moment, Wang remembered the egg in his bag, pulled it out and held it over his head.

"Is this what you lost?" he asked and raised the egg higher

Surprised, the dragon approached him and then asked: "What do you want?"

"I want you to promise me that if I give you this egg, you will leave and never come back here".

After thinking for a while, the Dragon consented and was given the egg. He immediately left the cave and flew to a place far away from humans. Soon the news reached the king and he rejoiced and asked that Wang would be brought into the palace and that he would be well fed. Then, as he had promised, he made Wang his successor and soon Wang married the princess. Finally there was peace in the kingdom and everyone could move freely without fear of the Dragon. And so from that day on, Wang was called the Dragon Emperor.

Summary:
Not all disputes can be resolved with violence, sometimes we need to seek free violent ways to resolve disputes. Wang knew that, which is why he managed to resolve the dispute between the kingdom and the Dragon without them fighting. We should prefer peace, not violence.

OSCAR

Oscar was a child who lived with his mother and father in a big city, and always found it difficult to sleep at night. He hated to sleep, and every time he was asked to sleep, he wasn't happy.

One night his mother was preparing him for bed.

"If you don't sleep, you won't grow up to be a pretty young man," his mother said as she bathed him. "Time to go to bed is good for you. I'm not tired and nighttime is boring, Mom. Sleep time ruins everything. The day is better because you can play more, play outdoors, be active and play video games," Oscar told mom. " Although I am tired, I am not so tired to sleep, I am never tired when I play".

"Young man, you have no choice", his mother scolded him. "You must go to bed".

Oscar went into his room and jumped on his bed. He had nothing to do but stare at the ceiling. He sighed and said.

"I'd like to do something fun".

He looked around in his room, looking for an object to play with. He saw an old wooden toy that had the shape of an elf, he took it and thought to himself saying: "I can play with this for now".

He turned the back of the wooden toy and there was faint writing on the back. He brought the toy closer to his eyes to read the words.

"Rub me twice with fabric," Oscar read.

"I can do it," he said to himself.

He took a strip of his pajamas and rubbed the wooden toy twice, but was disappointed when nothing happened. He thought the toy was about to start singing or moving. He dropped the toy in anger.

"It was a waste of time," he said.

Just then, the room lit up, and there was a strong wind in the room. The light and wind formed a portal.

"What is this?" Oscar said very frightened.

The wind and the light were very strong and they sucked Oscar. Oscar could not understand what was happening as he fell more and more into the portal.

Eventually he fell on a huge, fluffy, pink mushroom; he got up and tried to figure out where he was. He could see a line of big mushrooms everywhere.

"What is this place?" he thought out loud.

"You're here," said a voice.

Surprised, Oscar jumped, at the sound of his voice, turned to face whoever had that voice and his look met a little green elf, sitting on a mushroom next to him. It looked just like the old wooden toy he had rubbed.

"What are you?" he said with a trembling voice.

"What am I?" asked the surprised elf.

"Yeah, what are you?" Oscar asked with a brave face.

"You summoned me," replied the elf.

"When? I didn't do such a thing !" Oscar said.

"Yes, you did. Remember when you rubbed the old wooden toy?" said the elf.

"Oh, I see," replied Oscar. "I didn't mean to summon you, I was just following the instructions on the back. I didn't even know there was a toy like that in my room !" Oscar added.

The little green elf stared at him for a while before saying:

"I appear to children who have trouble sleeping at night and you have trouble sleeping at night. That's why I was in your room, it's my job to give the kids some time to have fun before they sleep," said the elf with a smile.

 "Where is this place then?" Oscar asked looking around.

"Welcome to the land of the game. All we do here is play and there are no nights" said the elf. " My name is Maleek the Elf, at your service".

"Wow! My name is Oscar. But there are only great mushrooms here!" Oscar said, without being impressed.

"They are our means of transport to the city." said the elf laughing. "Let me show you".

The little green elf began to jump on mushrooms, which were very soft and bouncy and were all straight into a single row leading somewhere.

"Don't stand there. Come with me". The elf called Oscar.

Oscar reached him and began to jump from one mushroom to another. He felt good as the breeze brushed against his face. He began to laugh as he jumped.

"This is funny," he said.

After a while they landed on a soft path and at the end of the path there was a bunch of green leaves covering what appeared to be a wall.

"What's behind it?" Oscar asked pointing at the leaves.

"This is the land of games," replied the elf.

Both walked towards the wall, the elf moved the leaves, and behind them was a beautiful city.

"Wow" said Oscar.

"Welcome," said the elf as they both entered the city.

Oscar had never seen a place like this before. There were different colors of chess pieces, of different sizes.

"This is chess land," explained the elf.

"Are there only chess games here?" Oscar asked.

"Yes, this is their city".

"Hey, be careful!" said a moving piece of chess.

"Excuse me!" said Oscar. "Wow is a chess piece that speaks and walks".

"Who is this, Maleek"? the chess asked.

"This is Oscar, he has trouble sleeping," replied Maleek.

"Oh, I see," said the chess.

"Nice to meet you," said Oscar.

"You stepped on me".

"Excuse me !"

"We have to solve this by playing chess," said the chess piece. "If you win, I'll let you continue into town".

"I don't want to," Oscar said.

"You must. You have no choice or you won't let us pass," said the elf to Oscar.

"Okay then" Oscar agreed. The chess piece placed itself on the ground and they both started playing. The king of chess, the queen and the knights could move alone without anyone's help.

"You chased my king, my friend," Oscar said unhappily.

"I doubt you'll win, I know every move of this game, because I'm the game," bragged the chess piece.

"The game is not over. You have to checkmate my queen to win," Oscar answered bravely. Minutes later:

"Checkmate !" Oscar happily exclaimed.

"This is not possible" the chess piece said shocked. "I have never been beaten in this game".

"He is really a smart boy," said the elf.

"Yes, yes he is", agreed on the chess piece.

And so the chess allowed Oscar and the elf to pass. They came across a very slippery road:

"I can't walk straight," Oscar continued to slide down the road.

"That's the idea," said the elf. "Just hold your leg straight and the road will slide you straight into the next town".

"Is this the way to the next city?" Oscar asked.

"Yes, just like big mushrooms".

They both slipped into a wall and stopped.

"We're here," the elf announced.

"What city is this?" Oscar asked.

"You'll find out soon," replied the elf.

They entered the city. It was full of different types of racing cars of different colors.

"How nice!" Oscar said. "Can I drive one?"

"Yes, but you have to ask permission of the car you want to drive," said the elf.

"Hey Maleek, who's your friend?" asked the car, watching Oscar.

"Hi Red! It's Oscar," replied the elf.

"I've never seen a talking racing car before," said Oscar.

"Well, now you have," he said.

"I wondered if I could let Oscar guide you," Maleek asked.

"Of course, but he has to race against another car while he drives," Red replied.

"Will anyone else drive the other car?" Oscar said.

"No, but I'll let you control me when you drive me," said Red. "But it's hard to beat a car that can drive itself".

"I play a lot with racing cars, I know how to run with a car," Oscar said.

"Very well then," said Red. "Let's begin".

Red called the other race cars.

"Let's have a race," he said.

"Why not !" Green answered, driving towards them.

"But the boy here will guide me," said Red.

The game was set and the finish line was 30 km from the starting line. All the land of the cars was there to watch the race. They all sang and cheered for the green car. None of them thought Oscar would win the race.

"One, two, three, go!" cried the speaker of the race.

Green left as quickly as possible, while Oscar and Red were still on the starting line.

"What are you waiting for?" said Red. "Guide me!"

"I don't know what to do. You're different from the cars I know," Oscar answered.

"Just press the red button to the left of the steering wheel".

Oscar did it and the car moved. Red gave him instructions on what to do and soon they reached Green. Seeing how close they were to him, Green threw sharp objects on the street.

"Take this !" Green said.

"Turn left," Red told Oscar. He did and they were able to escape sharp objects.

Red and Oscar overtook Green and ran ahead to get to the finish line before him, shocking every car in the country.

"Yes, we did it!"

"Yes, we did it!" replied Red.

They were surrounded by every car in the country, while everyone congratulated them.

"You did a good job," said the elf.

Oscar and the elf left the land of the cars and continued on their way.

"Where are we going next?" Oscar asked when they came to another wall.

"It's time for you to go home," said the elf. "Once you cross this wall you will be in your room".

"Thank you for a fun evening," Oscar replied. "I'm tired enough to sleep. I won't forget this day".

"You have to go to bed by 8:30 if you want to see me again," said the elf.

"Of course I will," Oscar said before crossing the wall and arriving in his room. He turned back and the wall was gone. The night was eventful and he was tired enough to want to sleep. He lay down on his bed smiling and before he knew it, he was sleeping deeply.

FRED LEARNS A NEW WAY OF SLEEPING

Fred didn't like staying up late, so he loved going to bed early. His father always said "early in bed to get you up early, it makes you strong and healthy". Fred loved to listen to his father's lullabies. His favorite was:

Little boy blue, come blow your horn,

The sheep's in the meadow, the cows in the corn.

Where is the little boy who looks after the sheep?
He's under the haystack, fast asleep

He always missed his father when he was away, because his father traveled a lot. His father ran a restaurant in the next town, so sometimes it was hard to see him.

Fred's friends always asked him how he could always be active at school and he said, "Well, I fall asleep early and this makes my body well-rested".

Fred also loved to play the piano because he said it sounded sweet when the right keys were pressed. He had a dog named Bell and sometimes he cuddled it when he wanted to go to bed.

One night, Fred was on the swing outside his house when he noticed a car parking in front of a house that had recently emptied out in front of his.

"It could be our new neighbors," he thought out loud.

He noticed a man and his wife with three children getting out of the car while a moving truck stopped in front of them.

"They are definitely our new neighbors and that child seems to be my age," he thought.

He stopped swinging and came home.

"Mom, we have new neighbors," he shouted to his mother who was in the kitchen making dinner.

"Okay, honey, why don't you go say hello?" his mother said.

"You mean just me? Can't we go together?" he asked.

"Well, then you'll have to wait until I'm done," said his mother. Fred had agreed to wait until his mother finished making dinner, since she was almost done. He went upstairs to take a bath and got changed putting on his favorite trousers.

"Did you change your clothes?" his mother asked surprised when she saw him coming down the stairs.

"The first impression matters, right?" said Jerry with a smirk on his face.

"Yes, actually," his mother smiled.

They both went to their new neighbors' house and said goodbye. Fred had met Alex who was the same age and was the last son of the family. They had to get to know each other better.

They found out Alex was going to go to the same school Fred attended, so they were pretty excited. Fred and Alex got along, and Fred thought it would be nice to go to school and get back together. The fact that they were both in the same class made them happy.

Fred would sometimes share his bedtime stories with Alex whenever he needed them and Alex would always return the favor. Together they relaxed their muscles with swimming courses three times a week. The most important thing was that they both enjoyed their naps. " That little rest during the day helps a lot," Alex's mom used to say.

 Fred always wondered how Alex could sleep the nights his father was out of town, because he couldn't sleep early.

"How can you sleep when your father is not there to read stories or sing for you?" Fred had asked on his return from school on a cool afternoon.

"Well, my mother does it for me, not my father".

"Okay, so how do you do it when she's not there?" Fred asked again and corrected himself.

"Most of the time I only listen to quiet, calm music," Alex answered.

"Music? Seriously? I thought it just made you stay awake". Fred had asked surprised.

"Well, it depends on what you listen to. To some people music is relaxing. Not all music is made for dancing".

"Great, I haven't heard or listened to any song that would relax me, do you have any suggestions?" Fred asked.

"Well, you should come later with your phone, I'll show you some of them." Alex answered Fred when they arrived at the side of the road where they had separated going in opposite directions.

"All right then," said Fred.

Fred came home and asked his mother how she felt about listening to music to sleep.

"It's really nice, but it all depends on what you like, baby".

"What do you mean what I like, Mom?" Fred asked.

"Well, some people listen to hard rock to relax and sleep, some listen to country music, some listen to hip pop, some listen to classic music. So it all depends on your preferences," said his mother.

"Oh okay, well I don't like anything hard or loud, I love something calm. Let's see what Alex has in store for me before," Fred concluded.

Fred went to Dave's house that night after his nap.

"Well, we have to try it this evening, I guess," thought Fred to himself as he was going through the songs he'd gotten from Alex.

In the evening, Fred turned on his music player and left it on as he went to bed. The music he was listening to made him feel relaxed. The sound had spread through the air and had made the whole room calm.

"Perfect," said Fred as he closed his eyes and fell asleep.

Joe and Two Maloy Teeth

Joe Fink and his partner, Two Maloy Teeth, moved their herd of cows across the Old West to Chicago along with Miss Angela Hale, a journalist who wanted to learn how to drive a herd. Joe and Two Teeth had found a rich man down in Chicago who wanted to buy the herd and that would allow him to build a school in their town of Boise.

"If you have to learn how to drive a herd, I think you'll want to start with how to ride a horse, Miss," said two teeth to Angela as he rode towards her.

She smiled, a little embarrassed, but at least there was someone who wanted to teach her something.

"The West is no place for a lady like you, you shouldn't be here," Joe used to tell her, making Angela think he had issues with her.

As they marched further west, the clouds began to change and soon there was a heavy downpour.

"We need to find a place to camp, the flood will slow us down," Joe told Two Teeth, who had Angela next to him.

"All right, I'd better go ahead and look for a good place".

Two teeth rode away and came running back a few minutes later, faster than when he left.

"Joe, we have a huge problem. Cow hunters, and they're heading this way. I think they saw me."

Joe turned to look at Angela's face. He knew she was scared.

"Well, if you want to learn how to drive a herd, you have to make sure you get a visit from cow hunters once in a while. We ride south, then, in this way we will try to bypass them," said Joe.

They rode in the heavy rain and could not see clearly through the rain. Suddenly the rain stopped and they found themselves in a forest.

"Where is this place?" asked Angela, amazed by the beauty of the forest.

"Well, Miss, where we are shouldn't be the problem, but who we run from should be. Let's get some rest, we will leave at first light", said Joe taking the saddle off his horse.

Two teeth, the next morning, he was awakened by the sound of his horse running away. He sat on the floor of the cave watching helplessly as it galloped away.

"Was it your horse?" asked Joe, rubbing his sleep from his eyes.

"I think so, something must have scared him. I have to go get him".

Just then there was a loud sound that came from outside and almost threw them back to the ground. Angela jumped up from where she lay and ran out of the cave with Joe and Two teeth behind her.

"Holy Mother of Christ, in the name of heaven, what is that? Tell me I'm not seeing it right now." Two teeth said when he noticed that they had spent the night with a family of dinosaurs.

"This friend is a dinosaur, and this group of dinosaurs is harmless. We simply found the land of the dinosaurs." Angela said, and walked towards them astonished.

"Well, I think we should pack, because I'm not going to be on any dinosaur's breakfast menu." He said, Two teeth running back into the cave.

"But they are not carnivores, they are kind and can be tamed", Angela called him back.

"Yeah, okay, did they tell you or was it written on their foreheads? You will not expect me to tame a dinosaur, you will expect me to flee from it", answered Two teeth coming out already with the bags packed.

"Well, I hope you know you still have no horse, mate. You mean you will walk to Chicago?" asked Joe trying in every way not to cross the gaze of his partner.

"Seriously, why do you have to remind me?"

"Because I'm the only one who cares about you, and I'm just trying to bring you back to reality. Either you tame one or you walk, your choice".

"I'll help you, Two Teeth" offered Angela with a big smile on her face.

"Oh, that's sweet of you," he replied, making a nervous grin.

Hours later they rode back on the road from which they had arrived, after Two teeth had successfully tamed one of the dinosaurs with Angela's help. They called him Patchy.

"Why in the world did you call him Patchy?" asked Joe.

"Because we felt attracted to each other very quickly, don't you get it? Attracted to Patchy," he answered, smiling for his creativity.

"Don't you think you should mean attached instead of attracted?" suggested Angela.

"Well, it's my dinosaur and my horse, so I decide how it got its name, okay?" Two teeth concluded riding away.

As they approached the entrance, they noticed that the raiders had camped just outside the entrance, and so they made a plan. Two teeth with his new friend came out first. Seeing the dinosaur the raiders ran away faster than they could, in different directions, forgetting they arrived with horses. Two teeth could not stop laughing because he had never seen a human run as fast as those raiders. Then the trio, with their new friend, marched forward with the herd of cows to Chicago.

Joe and Two Teeth finally sold the herd and built the school that their town had always wanted and Miss Angela was happy to have joined their journey. In the end she had learned a few things about leading a herd and also how to ride a horse, but above all she had discovered the lost land of the dinosaurs.

Summary:

When you have a purpose to reach, always be determined and do not let obstacles come between you and your goal. Remember, when obstacles start to show, you're on the right path.

HONESTY

Charlie sat on his bed, crying. Frankie did it again. He ate the cake that Mom left in the refrigerator and said Charlie had done it. It wasn't the first time he'd escaped something like this, every time he'd done something wrong, he'd always find a way to pin it on Charlie.

"I didn't do it, Mom, I swear I didn't do it".

He was always crying, but that didn't help because Frankie could always get proof that Charlie did it. Frankie had this big victory smile on his face because nothing gave him more joy than watching Charlie pay for something he hadn't done, and so Charlie vowed to prove that his brother had always been dishonest.

One night, their mother was on the night shift and Charlie was sleeping when he was suddenly awakened by a noise he heard in the hallway. He got out of bed to check and heard the noise again, this time from the kitchen. He snuck into a kitchen corner and saw Frankie rummaging through a bucket of ice cream that mom had bought the day before. In silence, he ran up the stairs and slipped out of the window of his room at the back of the house; he found the path to the control switch and turned off the lights throughout the house.

Meanwhile, Frankie sat in the dark kitchen, scared as a mouse.

"Hello, is there anyone?" he cried, hoping that Charlie would answer. Suddenly the back door opened and then there was a loud laugh.

"Arrgh!!!!," Frankie screamed and waited to hear Charlie's footsteps go down the stairs to control him, but there was nothing.

"Who are you?" Frankie wondered, not sure why he asked that question.

"I'm the ghost of ice cream and I'm here to get you, since you haven't been honest."

"Please don't take me," Frankie begged with his eyes closed

"I won't catch you on one condition: if you never lie on your brother Charlie again."

"I promise you, I will never do it again".

"Make sure you tell your mother the truth and not just the truth, but the whole truth or I'll come back for you. Now get out before I change my mind," Charlie said. He saw Frankie running up the stairs in his room screaming and crying at the same time. Charlie came down from where he was hiding and laughed: he had never seen Frankie so scared in his life, he was very sure that he would enjoy that moment for a long time.

"Charlie, Charlie, who ate the ice cream I left in the fridge?" His mother asked the next morning, surprised to see the empty ice cream bucket.

"I didn't do it, Mom," Charlie answered as he went down the stairs to meet her in the kitchen.

"Charlie, I hope you're not lying to me right now!" she asked, not convinced.

"Seriously, Mom, I didn't do it".

"Mom, I did it, and I wasn't honest with you. The truth is, I'm also responsible for the previous things," Frankie said as he walked into the kitchen with his head down.

"What do you mean young man?" his mother asked, angry and confused.

"Speaking honestly, he didn't do anything. It's always been me, and I always end up blaming Charlie," Frankie said.

She felt guilty for not believing Charlie and for all this time he had been innocent. So, hearing what Frankie said, she felt guilty because she'd always believed Frankie while Charlie was the honest one. So she promised to reward him, and as for Frankie, she grounded him for three weeks and made him do all the chores himself.

Summary:

To be honest, whether people believe in you or not, it really pays. Don't stop being as honest as Charlie, because in the end the truth will always prevail.

ADAM AND MR. ICEBERG

It was the last day of school, and Adam was so happy that winter break was coming. He couldn't wait to go back to Alaska to visit his grandmother, his friend Toby and Mr. iceberg. He was sitting in class and remembered all the fun they had last winter and all the stories of Mr. iceberg, and this made him eager to visit again.

"What are your plans for your holiday, Adam?" Andrew asked, putting his books in his backpack.

"I'm going to Alaska to visit my grandmother and also my friends who I missed so much, especially Toby" Adam replied with excitement in his eyes, "And you, what are your plans?"

"Well, I'm going to Florida to see my aunt. I'm going to visit her for the first time", Andrew answered.

"I think we'll meet after winter break then," said Adam as soon as the bell rang, and ran out to meet his mother waiting outside the school to pick him up.

Adam awoke early on the day he was supposed to travel, very excited. He washed and brushed his teeth before going down for breakfast. He had already packed the day before to not forget anything. Mum served pancakes and orange juice and as soon as they were done, Adam, with his bag, ran straight to the taxi waiting outside to take them to the airport.

Arrived in Alaska, the grandmother was already waiting outside the house with Toby next to her. "Grandma!!" Adam shouted, excited to see her. He ran to her and gave her a hug.

"I missed you so much, Grandma!"

"Me too, it's good to see your face again," she said smiling before kissing him on the cheek. Adam and Toby said goodbye before they came into the house.

The next day, Adam and Toby were playing out with other kids when Adam asked,

"How is Mr. iceberg? I'm looking forward to seeing him".

"The last time we met he was fine, but I haven't seen him in the last few weeks," Toby answered, and his expression changed. " It's not like him not to show up when we have an appointment," Toby added.

"Well, if that's the case, I think we should pay him a visit tomorrow. I'm worried about him now," Adam said, hoping that Mr. iceberg would be okay.

The next day they went to see Mr. iceberg, as planned, and he always showed up near the edge of the lake. But just like Toby had said the day before, Mr iceberg didn't show up, and that made the kids even more concerned. They came back the next day and the day after and still he didn't show up. On the fourth day, they sat by the lake wondering what might have happened to Mr. iceberg.

"This is not like him. He knew we were coming to see him and yet he didn't show up. But why didn't he show up? This is making me worry," Adam said confused.

"I don't know, but I just pray nothing bad happened to him," Toby said drawing on the ice. At that very moment, Mr. iceberg came out, but he looked different and did not notice the boys sitting on the lakeshore. Adam and Toby were happy and surprised to see him. Mr Iceberg had changed a lot, shrinking a lot. They called his name together.

"Mr. iceberg!"

Surprised, he turned to see Adam and Toby standing on the lakeside smiling at him and so he turned and went to them.

"It's good to see you again guys," he said when he approached them.

"You too, Mr. iceberg. But what happened to you? You've changed and you don't seem well," Adam said approaching him.

"You've shrunk a lot, what happened?" Toby asked, surprised to see a huge difference.

"Well, I'm not feeling very well and that's why I'm shrinking," he replied.

"It's not like you to be sick, what's the problem?" Toby asked, worried.

"Well, the climate is affecting me, and secondly, those industries on the other side of the lake are polluting the lake. The chemical content of the waste they dispose of in the lake kills aquatic animals and also reduces my ice melting it".

"So how can we help?" Adam asked, frightened that one day Mr. iceberg might disappear.

"First, industries should learn other ways to dispose of their chemicals, and not release them into the lake and then the smoke coming out of their industries must be reduced. Secondly, people should learn to take care of the surrounding environment and stop throwing harmful objects and substances around and especially around the lake. This would help us a lot".

"All right, we'll help you, we promise," Toby said.

"Yes, we will, we won't let you down," Adam told Mr iceberg, who watched them run home.

A few weeks later, they returned to visit Mr. iceberg and saw him already waiting, whiter than before, and he was delighted to see them.

"Hi, kids" he said.

"Hi, you look better now, unlike when you looked like an old man," Adam joked.

"Well, thank you for saving us, me and the aquatic animals. We are grateful".

"No, we just did our part and people did theirs and so they deserve your thanks more than we do," Toby said with a smile.

"Well, now that I'm better and healthy. I think it's time to tell you about the time I went to the Arctic region. Then I have much more to say. Come on, this will be very funny", said Mr. Iceberg as the children climbed on him and he took them down the lake telling them stories.

Summary

We should learn to keep our environments clean, so as to help animals survive and also by helping ourselves to live a

MONKEY AND CROCODILE

Once upon a time there was a monkey who lived in a tree near the shore of a river. He was a fruit merchant and the best in the business. He sometimes traveled far by sea to buy most of the fruit. So he had a great variety of fruit and this made him well known. One day, he had to embark on a voyage by sea to buy some fruit and so he left his home early as usual. When he arrived at the port, he realized he had left his ticket at home. He ran home to get it, but by the time he got back, the ship had sailed. Dissatisfied and frustrated he returned home and sat down near the river bank crying. "Hello Monkey, why are you crying?" a deep voice asked. The monkey jumped to his feet as a crocodile approached him.

"I didn't mean to scare you, I'm just worried," Crocodile added knowing that Monkey was scared.

"I missed the boat that was supposed to take me to buy fruit and now I can't buy it to sell it".

"It's really sad but I can help you by transporting you and bringing you back for a good price," said the crocodile.

"So, what's your price?" asked the monkey, glad to hear that the crocodile wanted to help.

"You'll pay me with half the bag of your juicy fruit after every trip".

"Done", said monkey and immediately jumped on the back of the crocodile. Immediately they were on their way.

Soon after, the monkey and the crocodile had become best friends. They traveled by sea and returned faster than the monkey expected and this helped the monkey to expand, because he put the money needed for the ticket to buy more fruit. So one-day crocodile came home to his wife after he had been on one of those trips and brought back fruit as usual.

"What's wrong, dear?" he asked his wife, surprised that she didn't come out to greet him as usual.

"Every day you travel with a monkey and end up coming home with fruit. Aren't you tired of eating fruit?" she asked furiously.

"Well, I am, but what do you want me to do? We have a deal." crocodile answered.

"Deals can be broken, right?"

"Yes, but what exactly are you suggesting?" asked crocodile, not sure what to expect.

"It's time we started eating meat. I miss it, and to tell you the truth, we're flesh-eating reptiles, not fruit-eating reptiles." She said with a little anger in her voice. "Find a way to convince him to go out to sea with you and then finish it. I want monkey stew and he's what we need." He added.

"But he is my friend." He cried devastated.

"And I am your wife and should be your priority. I need monkey stew." she insisted.

The crocodile was devastated but had no choice.

Then one day he and monkey embarked on another journey and crocodile had decided to implement his wife's idea of killing monkey. During the crossing, the crocodile changed the road and headed into the open sea. The monkey immediately realized that there was something wrong, but he was not sure, and then asked, "Why do we change course?"

"I just wanted us to explore a little," he said, crocodile, and gave a weak smile to a monkey. After about fifteen minutes monkey was sure that something was wrong.

"We're not exploring, are we?"

"I'm sorry, man, but I have to do this for my wife."

Monkey got scared and thought of a way to escape the danger at hand.

"I understand, my friend, but if you kill me without the heart and kidneys in their place, you won't enjoy the stew. Take me home and let me take them, then you can take me home to your wife alive."

Monkey did not believe his fortune when the crocodile accepted the idea and brought him home. As soon as the monkey hit the ground, he quickly ran up a tree and said, "I actually thought we were friends, but now I know we're not. There will be no monkey stew for your wife today. Go away and never come back." said the angry monkey.

At that point, Crocodile realized he'd been cheated and came home empty-handed.

A BOY CALLED TYRESE

Once lived a child named Tyrese, who lived in an old wooden house with his mother. Their home was at the end of the streets and everyone in town knew how poor they were. Tyrese and his mother had no food to eat and their clothes were torn and worn. It saddened him to see his mother struggling to feed them both, but they were as happy as they could. Tyrese loved to sing and always had a guitar that his mother had bought for him. One Saturday morning Tyrese and his friends John and Peter thought to go to the city fair: Tyrese wanted to make some money singing at the fair with his guitar.

He got up early that morning, and went straight to his mother who was already awake and ready to go sell her famous homemade cake.

"Good morning, mother," said Tyrese

"Good morning, honey," said his mother. "Well, I left some cake for you".

The cake was all they ate, it was all they had to eat but he didn't complain.

"I'll put it in my bag and eat it later at the fair," Tyrese replied.

"Have fun at the fair," his mother said as she kissed him on the forehead.

"I will," he answered and ran away.

Tyrese, John and Peter met at the park as planned.

"You really came with your guitar! To do what?" said John to Tyrese.

"I told you I would play at the fair today, I want to make some money," Tyrese replied.

"But we have already told you that we will pay for any game or ride you want at the fair. We are here to have fun," objected Peter.

"I appreciate that, but I want to help my mother with the money I'm going to make at the fair," Tyrese said.

"Do you really want to be like your music idol Chris," Peter said. "Do you know that he started his musical career singing at community fairs? But I still think you should leave your guitar and have fun with us," he added.

Seeing that they couldn't convince him otherwise, John and Peter let him go with the guitar on their way to the fair. As they were walking towards the fair, they spotted an old man standing on a bench in the street. The old man looked weak and tired.

"Look at that man," John said to his friends. " Will he be okay?"

"He must have had too much to drink. I'm sure he's drunk," Peter said.

"Yes, he must be a drunk," agreed John. "My mom always tells me to stay away from men like that," he added.

"Help me," the old man called the boys.

"Let's help him," Tyrese begged his friends.

"No, you don't need to help or care for a stranger," said John.

"Call 911," whispered the old man.

"Come on," Peter said.

"Go ahead, see you later," said Tyrese.

John and Peter left Tyrese alone with the man. Being a good-hearted boy, Tyrese took the old man's phone and called 911. He also followed the old man in the ambulance while the medical staff took them to the hospital.

"Is he your grandfather?" said the doctor who took care of the old man.

"No, it's not. I saw him on the street and I decided to help him," Tyrese replied.

"You're a very kind-hearted guy. If you hadn't called, he would have died of a heart attack," the doctor said.

"Here's his phone. You may need it to contact his family," Tyrese said as he delivered the old man's phone to the doctor.

"Thank you, we'll contact them".

"And this is my address in case he needs more help. I am willing to help him," said Tyrese by giving a piece of paper to the doctor.

It was already evening when Tyrese left the hospital. It was obvious that he could no longer go to the fair. He walked home, he knew he had to go home and be with his mother, but he was a little sad that he didn't earn the money he wanted to give his mother.

It had been a week since the accident and Tyrese were always wondering what had happened to the old man, hoping that his family had gone to pick him up. It was a hot Sunday afternoon and Tyrese was ready to spend the whole day at home with his mother.

"Tyrese," he heard his mother scream.

"Yes, Mom," he answered running to the front door.

He was shocked to see the old man standing out with his music idol Chris next to him. Tyrese ran up to them screaming at the top of his lungs and gave the old man a big hug.

"You are well!" Tyrese said in tears.

"Yes, I am. And it's all thanks to you," replied the old man with a smile.

"Thanks for helping my father," Chris said.

"Father?" answered Tyrese in shock.

"Yes, Chris is my son".

"Thank you very much. My father almost had a heart attack and you were there to help him", said Chris. "The doctor told us everything, gave us the piece of paper with your address and I wanted to come to reward you for caring about my father".

"What are they talking about?" said Tyrese's mother.

"Let me explain," Chris said.

Chris explained everything to Tyrese's mom.

"He has a very good heart," she said.

"I learned from you," said Chris.

Chris and his father bought a house for Tyrese and his mother, sent him to school and enrolled him on his son's music label. Tyrese became a star just because he took care of someone and lived happily ever after with his mother.

Summary:
We should all learn to show kindness and compassion, regardless of who we are or who we

show kindness and compassion to. In the end, surely we will have rewards in return. If we grow up with compassion and kindness, the world will surely be a better place.

REYNA'S CURLS

Reyna was a black girl with curls, but she always felt uncomfortable going to school with her curls, because they were a lot and the other kids in the school always laughed when they saw her coming. Sometimes, during break time, she sat next to the swing in the playground, alone, while the others played together. Playing alone wasn't fun, and she really wanted to join the others but she didn't want to be laughed at again because of her hair, and felt like she had the worst hair in the world. Not that she hated her hair, but the teasings of the other children in her class made her feel bad. She was once compared to a sheep by Jason, a boy in her class. Reyna went home crying to her dad. "I hate my curls, Dad," she said when she entered the room. "Hey, why do you say that, my Princess?" she asked and sat down next to her. "Some kids in my class keep calling me names and they don't want to play with me because of my big curls and today I was compared to a sheep by a guy named Jason," she said, very sad. "Well, I know you're not a sheep, but my daughter, and it doesn't matter how they see your curls, because I love them and they make my little princess beautiful," he said, raising her up to cheer her up, and she laughed. But that didn't stop Reyna being teased more and the worst thing was when she finally got her curls cut because of the chewing gum that the kids had put in them. Reyna promised never to let them grow back again. Weeks later there was a new girl in the class who had curls bigger than Reyna's, but what surprised Reyna was that this little girl was already making friends with the kids in the class, and finally she started looking for a way to finally be able to talk to her. Eventually one day she did it, the last day of school before a short holiday. Reyna saw her sitting alone waiting for her parents to pick her up. She walked up to her and said: "Hi, I'm Reyna". The new girl turned around and saw Reyna smiling and smiled back before answering: "Hi, I'm Julia". "I'm in your class and I was wondering if I could ask you a few questions". "OK," said Julia, "what is it about, Reyna?". "How do you feel about your curls?" Reyna asked. "I feel good about them," Julia answered, not surprised by the question. " I can see that you're having problems here at school". "Well, yeah. The kids in our class forced me to get rid of mine, but they're treating you differently. How did you do that?" "Wow, you used to have curls?". "Well, yeah, but the constant teasing was too much". "I bet they put gum in your hair," said Julia.

"How did you know?" Reyna asked, wondering how she knew. "Well, they did the same thing to me at my old school, and I cried for a whole week. I even refused to go to school again, and one day my grandmother paid us a visit. I told her everything that happened, and all she did was laugh at first. Then she finally said, "Well, I know for sure those kids did this to your hair because they don't have curls. But you do, and they're jealous. Get Mr Travis, who lives across the street, he's bald, isn't he? But he still goes around minding his own business every morning, even though the kids laugh at him, and he doesn't care. So be like him, and cheer up, my dear Julia, and know that it does not matter how many times you cut your hair because they will grow back again. You just have to understand that your curls are part of you, you can't get rid of them, and instead of cutting them, you have to learn to live with them and show the kids at your school how beautiful your curls are and bring them with pride. Remember that they are part of your beauty". And since then I haven't let anyone or anything they've done to me bother me, Julia said smiling. "Thanks for the chat Julia, see you back at school", Reyna said leaving with a smile, not feeling worried anymore about getting the curls to grow back. And she was also happy to make a new friend. When they went back to school after their vacation, Reyna returned with her curls that had grown back, and was more proud of them than ever. "Yes, you grew them back, that's what I was talking about," said Julia when she saw Reyna enter the classroom in the new academic year. " Yes, you inspired me, and thank you for helping me," said Reyna giving her a smile. "You're welcome, now let's show them the beauty of our curls," Julia said, responding to the smile. Since then, every time Reyna looks in the mirror she smiles, because they make her feel like she's herself again. In the end, she feels good about herself for the first time. Reyna and Julia became best friends and soon the other girls wanted to be friends. This made her happy and she finally felt great with her curls.

Summary:

Don't let people's opinions affect you. We are Who we chose to be because only you can decide yourself. People's opinions shouldn't always matter, what matters Is what you think of yourself and how you are yourself.

THE SLEEPING PRINCESS

Long ago lived a king and queen who every day said: "If only we had a child of our own!" But for a long time they had none. With them lived a boy named Adam who was very loyal to the king and queen. They treated him like a son and loved him very much.

One day, while the queen bathed in the spring, a frog came out of the water and said, "Your wish will be granted. Before a year has passed you will give birth to a daughter, because you have the purest of hearts and treat everyone with respect".

Since frogs are magical animals, it was no surprise that before a year passed the queen had a daughter. The child was so beautiful and sweet that the king could not restrain himself from joy. After the daughter's birth, the queen's attitude changed and she became dismissive and arrogant and began to treat her subjects as peasants. Her love for Adam disappeared and that made him so unhappy that he had to leave the castle to travel to another castle. One day the king prepared a great feast and invited all who were in his kingdom. He also invited the fairies, so that they could be kind and kind to the child. There were thirteen of them in his kingdom, but the queen secretly ordered that only twelve golden plates be prepared from which they could eat. So one of the fairies had to stay out. None of the guests felt sorry for this, but this enraged the 13th fairy.

There was a wonderful party and when it was over, the fairies presented the little girl with a magical gift. One fairy gave her virtue, another beauty and the third wealth and so on. After eleven fairies had passed, suddenly the thirteenth appeared. She was angry and wanted to show her resentment for being left out of the party. Without hesitation she declared aloud: "When she is fifteen years old, the princess will look into a mirror and when she sees her reflection she will fall dead and all who are in the castle will fall into a deep sleep".

Then without another word she turned and left the room.

The guests were horrified and the queen fell to the ground crying bitter tears for making such a wrong decision. The twelfth fairy, who had not yet expressed her desire, silently came forward. Her magic could not remove the curse but could mitigate it, as she said.

"No, your daughter will not die but she may be awakened by true love, by a person as pure as you were before changing, my queen".

With the years the promises of the fairies came true. All those who saw the girl could not help but love her.

The king and queen were determined to prevent the curse placed on the princess by the wicked fairy and issued an edict for which every mirror, throughout the kingdom, was destroyed. No one in the kingdom was allowed to speak of the curse placed on her because they didn't want her to worry or be sad.

On the morning of her 15th birthday, the princess woke up early, excited to be a year older. She wandered everywhere, looking into every room and every room at will, and eventually came to an old tower. She climbed up the narrow, winding stairs and reached a small door. A rusty key was in the lock and when she turned it the door opened wide.

In a small room sat an old woman with a spinning wheel, spinning the spindle, and behind her was a huge mirror. The old woman was deaf and had not heard the edict that all mirrors should be destroyed.

"Good morning, Grandma," said the princess, "What are you doing?"

"I'm spinning," said the old lady.

"What is that thing?" the princess asked, going by the beautiful mirror on the wall.

"It's a mirror," said the old lady, "don't you have one in your room?"

"No, this is the first time I've ever seen one in my life," said the princess.

She came over to take a closer look and suddenly saw her reflection in the mirror. At that moment she fell on the bed that was nearby and fell into a deep sleep.

The king, queen and servants had begun their morning habits and in the midst of the chores they all fell asleep. Around the castle began to grow a great hedge of wild roses. Every year it got taller until in the end you could see nothing more of the castle asleep.

There was a legend in the country about the beautiful sleeping princess, and how, from time to time, princes came and tried to make their way through the hedge to the castle. But this was impossible because of the thorns, which, as they were alive, seized them and did not let them through.

After five years, Adam returned to the country and heard an old man tell the story of the castle behind the hedge and the beautiful princess who had been sleeping for five years. He also felt that many princes had tried to cross it but none had succeeded and some had been trapped and had died.

Then Adam said, "I'm not afraid. I have to go see the princess asleep":

The good old man did everything he could to convince him not to go but he didn't listen. As he walked towards the hedge, the shrubs moved as they wanted and let him pass without injury.

In the courtyard Adam saw the horses and dogs lying asleep. When he entered the castle he also found servants asleep in the rooms. Next to the throne lay the king and queen who slept peacefully next to each other. In the kitchen the cook and the kitchen boy and the kitchen girl slept with their heads on the table.

The prince moved on. Everything was so quiet that he could feel his own breath. He finally reached the tower and opened the door, entered the little room where the princess slept. She lay there, and looked so beautiful that he could not take his eyes off her. He bent down and gave her a kiss. As soon as he touched her, she opened her eyes and smiled at him. Throughout the castle, everything and everyone woke up and looked at each other in amazement. When the king and queen found out it was Adam who saved them, they were sorry and asked for his forgiveness. Within a month

Adam and the princess were married and lived happily for the rest of their lives.

Summary:

Learn to give importance and extend your love to all those around you because you don't know where help will come from. Try not to be dismissive but calm and loving.

THE TRIPLETS

There once was a man named Mr. John. He was a very rich, kind and honest businessman, and he had a toy factory, where he made toys for children. She had three children who were twins named Paul, Peter and Patrick, who were nine years old. He had raised his children after his wife died in childbirth. He loved his children and gave them everything they wanted, but his children did not love each other and hated working together. That made Mr. John very worried and sad.

Paul, Peter and Patrick were special and had different talents. Paul was very good at music and was great with the piano. Peter was a genius, he could think faster than a normal kid, while Patrick was the fastest guy in the whole city. He had the ability to run faster than a lion. The three were really good with their talents and they were known in town for their special talents. Paul was in the church children's choir, Peter was the leader of the rocket science club at school, while Patrick represented the school at every racing event. The twins were all fine, but they never got along at home.

A bright Sunday morning, Mr. John had woken the boys and asked them to prepare for the church and had asked them to bathe together, so they would not be late for church.

"Dad, I can't bathe with them," Peter said. "Paul loves to sing in the shower and Patrick bathes so fast that he pours water everywhere".

"I don't want to bathe with any of them," Patrick added.

"But you are brothers, why don't you like working together?" asked Mr John.

"Dad, please, we don't want to bathe together," the triplets said together.

"Okay, I give up", said Mr. John and he had left the boys.

On his way down the stairs, his mother came into the house.

"Why the sad look?" she asked.

"It's the kids. They refuse to get along," he replied.

"Don't worry about that," she said.

"I can't. I think I need to do something before they completely hate each other".

"They're just children, they'll learn over time; plus you're doing a good job as a single parent".

"I know, but we still have to do something, Mom. It breaks my heart to watch them fight all the time," he said.

One day, the boys were sitting in the living room with their father, when he had received visitors from the bank. Mr. John had made a plan with them to make them come and, in front of the boys, tell him that they would sell the factory if he did not pay his debt.

"Two weeks is too little for me to repay you, give me more time," said Mr. John.

"Sorry sir, we can't do that, you only have two weeks," replied the visitor.

"Where do I get all that money in two weeks?" said Mr. John with a frowny face.

Although the three boys were all in the living room when the visitor came, Peter was the only one who understood what the visitor was talking about. He immediately asked his brothers to follow him to his room, after the visitors had left, which they did.

"Why did you call us here?" Patrick asked.

"Those men in the other room want to take everything from us".

"What are you talking about?" Paul asked.

"Dad owes the bank and if he doesn't pay in time we'll lose the house and the toy factory".

"What?" exclaimed Paul and Patrick.

"How do you know" Paul asked

"I was listening to them".

"How did you understand what they were saying?" Patrick said.

"I'm very smart, have you forgotten?" answered Peter.

"How will Dad take care of us, if they take the toy factory?" added Paul.

"I feel sorry for Dad, he always takes care of us, but all we did was make him sad," said Patrick.

"I wish there was something we could do," added Paul.

"Wait, I have an idea. What if we made money for Dad?" Peter said with a smile.

"How?" Paul asked.

"We must work together".

Paul, Peter and Patrick had an idea of how to help their father.

Their plan was to use their individual talents. Peter's brilliant plan was to create a new kind of toy and to make people know it. Paul and Patrick were supposed to have a musical event and a running event.

"But we are too young to do this," said Patrick.

"We'll go to Dad with our plan, he'll help us," Peter said.

Three days after the boys had gone to their father with their plan, Peter had already created a toy.

"We want to help you, Dad," said Paul.

"We were bad boys," added Patrick.

"No, boys, you weren't. Tell me about your plan," said Mr. John.

"I already have a toy that I made, and I want to show it on that day".

"In the meantime I will give a musical show where children can sing and have fun," Paul added.

"And I will give an event on the track where the kids will register and try to win one of the toys by running faster than me," said Patrick.

"Then let's do it!" replied Mr John.

Mr. John was delighted that his boys were finally working together; he hugged them tight and was delighted that they were willing to help him.

They had the toy, the music and the track race, there were a lot of guys who came for the show. There were games for the kids to play and lots of other fun activities. The children loved the toy that Peter had created and enjoyed the show that Paul and Patrick had put on. By the end of the show they had sold all the toys they had made and had enough money to pay off the bank.

"I'm sorry I was mean to both of you," Paul told both Peter and Patrick.

"Me too," Peter said.

"I feel so bad! We're brothers, so let's stop fighting and love each other," said Patrick as they hugged each other.

Their father started clapping behind them. "That's all I wanted," he said. Then he started telling them how he tricked them into thinking they were losing their house and the toy factory. The visitors who came were friends and he knew that Peter was smart enough to understand what they were saying. That's why he and his friend sat next to Peter while they were arguing, because he wanted to see them work together.

"We are not losing the house or the toy factory," said Mr. John. "I will take the money made today and put it in the bank for you. When the three of you are old enough, you can use the money", then he looked at them and said: "I am very proud of you three, come and give me a hug". They all rushed to hug their father with tears in their eyes.

"Working together was better than working alone," they said as they hugged each other.

"We agree," the boys said immediately.

After the show they had received awards in their schools and had many more friends of their age than before. Paul had started writing songs for the church's children's choir; Peter had continued to create things at the rocket science fair for children, while Patrick was to represent the country at an international children's competition.

Since then, the triplets had shared everything, shared clothes, shoes, food, everything they had, and had stopped being bad to each other. They had learned that life is easier when everyone shares with love.

Summary:

When we work together, we achieve a lot and save time and strength. Things are fine where there is unity. We should learn to work together.

RUBY REMEMBERS

After dinner, Ruby, the kitten, and little Sally were ready for bed. Ruby always told a bedtime story before they fell asleep.

"Hey, Ruby, I'm ready for today's story," said the excited little Sally while they were jumping into bed.

"All right, Sally".

"I'll tell you the story of when I was almost lost and I was found by Mr Smith," said Ruby.

"Well, I once lived in a great mansion with my owner, Mrs Doris. I had everything I ever dreamed of, food, milk and a room for myself. Above all, I had so much love, because Mrs Doris had no children, and I was treated like a princess.

One morning I woke up and realized that my milk plate was empty instead of being full of milk. Mrs Doris hardly forgot to fill my plate with milk every morning so I wondered what was wrong.

I quickly went to the kitchen to see if she was there, but she wasn't there, then I searched the whole house but I didn't see her.

"Could Mrs Doris have left without me?" I thought to myself. " Maybe she went to the grocery to get supplies," I thought out loud.

So I took a bottle of milk, sat on the table, poured it into my plate and drank while I waited for her to come back.

After eating I went to the living room to watch my favorite TV show, Kitty Rescue. Mrs. Doris and I used to enjoy watching it, it was our favorite show.

Later that night, Mrs Doris hadn't returned. I worried and wondered where she might have gone, because she never stayed out late. Just then I remembered that she said she would travel and that she wasn't sure when she would be back. Then I realized she might have left me.

"Oh, no! What did you do then?" Sally asked.

"Well, I ran to her room only to find that her suitcases were not there. That left me sad and confused.

"Oh, my God! Does that mean she traveled without you?" Sally asked with her paw on her mouth.

"Yes, I'm afraid so".

So I left the house hoping to find her, but I got lost on the road and couldn't find my way back.

I sat under a tree crying, having lost all hope and was also hungry when I saw a shadow approaching me.

I looked up and I saw a big, tall man. At first I was scared and I tried to run away but he held me, touched my fur coat and said, "Hello, kitten, what's your name?"

"I'm Ruby," I said, still scared.

"I am Mr Smith"; he replied.

"Why are you out here, sad and all alone?" he asked.

"My owner accidentally forgot me and left", I answered.

" And I went out to look for her but instead I got lost and I can't find my way home," I added almost crying.

"It's very sad, I know you're sad and hungry but don't worry. I'm taking you to a nice house," he said with a smile. " I'm from Kitty Rescue," added Mr Smith.

"Oh, really? It's our favorite show," I said excited and feeling sure I was safe. "You guys rock!"

"Oh, that's great Ruby. I'm glad you know about us and that you love our work," he said.

"You're my hero, Mr Smith!" I said happily.

Mr Smith smiled at me, carried me gently and walked down the road.

"So when I first got here, I never thought I could survive, and you helped me. Thank you, Sally, you really are a friend," said Ruby.

"Don't even say it, Ruby, anything for a mate. But you were really brave to go out looking for Mrs Doris," Sally said.

"Well, I know, but that's how I finally got here," said

Ruby.

"It's so sad, Ruby, but don't worry, I will always treat you like my princess," said little Sally with a smile on her face.

"Thanks Sally, I already feel like a princess," said Ruby. They hugged, then Sally kissed Ruby and said, "Goodnight, princess".

Weeks later, Ruby was awakened by the laughter of a familiar voice. Just then, Mr Smith walked towards her with someone behind him and said:

"Guess who came to take you home?"

He stepped to the side and Mrs Doris walked towards Ruby and took her in her arms.

"I missed you so much," she said.

"Me too," Ruby said with a smile.

As they were leaving, she remembered Sally and felt bad leaving her behind.

"Can't she come too, Mrs Doris? Please, she's my friend," Ruby prayed.

"Sure, and I'm glad you made new friends. So every time I travel you won't be alone".

"Thank you, Mrs Doris," answered Ruby.

And then Ruby and Mrs Doris and Sally went back to the mansion and lived happily together.

Summary:

We should learn to be accommodating and friendly. If Sally hadn't been friendly with Ruby, she wouldn't have had a new house Ruby would have been sad. So help someone today.

RETALIATION

One sunny day, at school, Trevor argued with one of his classmates; Jared.

Trevor was sent home for misconduct.

"Trevor, your teacher, just called me, you fought with another child again," cried Mrs. Trevor.

Trevor, as a seven-year-old boy, was too aggressive and arrogant. He was a boy without common sense, who had never used the phrase 'I am sorry' before. He never listened to his parents' advice, let alone his teachers' advice. He was always involved in the struggles at school and was well known at school as an annoying boy.

"It wasn't my fault, mom, he started it first and didn't mind her own business. Mom, he crossed the line and I had to teach him a lesson," Trevor answered, throwing the bag over the couch.

"No need to fight, Trevor, you should have tried to make peace".

"Come on! Mom, you didn't suggest that I should do that!" exclaimed Trevor, surprised to hear those things from his mother.

"What's wrong with all this, what's wrong with you leaving?"

"Everything, Mom. He wronged me, so he had to pay, and that's what I did, I made sure of it".

"You don't have to pay evil with evil, you have to learn to love those who have made bad things against you." answered Trevor's mom.

"But that's not right, Mom! Why should I repay evil with good?" Trevor asked his mother.

"This is because as human beings, we should love our neighbors as we love ourselves." she replied. " By the way, you never told me what did he do wrong?"

"There's nothing to say, Mom," he answered, grabbing his backpack and then ran up the stairs to his room.

Mrs Trevor sat on the couch with a worried face. She wasn't sure what to do, but she was afraid of one thing, and that was the fact that her son was getting out of hand. She had to do something! Of course she would!

The next day, Mrs. Trevor dropped Trevor off at school and noticed the way the other kids were staring at him. When Jared saw him walking towards his direction, he changed direction. She was so sad about it, she decided to have a chat with him when she got home from work.

"Did you apologize to Jared?" Mrs. Trevor asked after they finished dinner that night.

"No, for what?"

"You hurt him, Trevor. Didn't you notice the way the other students were staring at you? Jared even had to change direction when he saw you coming," she said.

"I didn't and he has to keep running".

"Trevor!", she cried. "You should learn to show love and support".

"How can I love children who hate me? Mom, kids at school get on my nerves all the time, so it's not possible," answered Trevor.

"Son, I know how you feel, but it's not good to pay evil with evil. What do you get out of being a bully? And if one day they would gang up against you, what would happen?" she asked.

"I don't understand what you're saying, Mom," he said confused.

"How would you feel if they joined together to beat you?"

"It would be unfair and I would feel bad, I would also feel hurt," answered Trevor.

"This is an honest answer, because it really is unfair to you, just as it is unfair to them now," said Mrs. Trevor.

"It's the same way those kids feel when you hit them, they feel hurt, sad and ashamed.", she added.

"I didn't know. But that doesn't mean they should continue to stand in my way," Trevor said.

"Beating your classmates won't stop them from upsetting you: it makes them hate you even more," answered Trevor's mom.

"What am I supposed to do, Mom?"

"You have to ignore them and let go of the things they do to you, because they're just trying to piss you off. They can't beat you, and they know it, so the only way to hurt you is to make you angry," said his mother.

"So, you mean I should ignore them? But everyone will think I'm weak and might start to see me as a chicken!"

"This is their opinion, and it doesn't matter. What matters is that you love your neighbor as you love yourself. Just look at Jesus in the Bible: with all the powers he had, he never used it against those who were evil, those who hated him or those who wanted him dead. Instead he continued to pray for them, to ask God to forgive their sins because he felt that they did not know what they were doing," his mother answered.

"Now I understand Mom, I love you so much!" Trevor said before hugging his mother.

Trevor had just realized that as long as he continued to retaliate, paying evil with evil, the other children will continue to cause him problems. The only way to avoid it is to love them, just as Jesus loves everyone here on earth; not by paying evil with evil, and by loving those who hate us.

Summary:
Not to retaliate doesn't make you weak, it makes you strong. Only a wise and strong person would know when to react and when not. Retaliation is not the best way to deal with things. Ask Trevor, now he knows.

SUZIE'S RAINBOW

Suzie loved playing outside with her friends, Rosy, Thelma, Brian and Bobby. Every day after school, she went to Thelma's house and, along with the others, played until Suzie's parents came to pick her up.

One Sunday morning it was raining hard and Suzie had planned to go play at Thelma's, but she was asked not to go outside.

"I will wear my coat and boots, Dad, and I will be careful," she prayed, promising it to his parents.

"Suzie, darling, there's no way you can go out and play in this rain. It's very dangerous, honey, but once the rain stops, you can go outside and play all the time you want. But for now you'll have to stay inside and play until the rain stops," replied her father. So their answer was still no. Suzie wasn't happy, and playing alone wasn't funny, but there had never been a time when she had been disobedient.

The rain continued for days and that made Suzie unhappy. For days, she couldn't go out to play with her friends, so she got tired of the rain. Then she asked his mother, "Mum, won't it stop raining?" with a tired look on his face.

"It will stop, dear, when the time is right, but I'm not sure when it will be. You know what, come over here and let me tell you a story about the rain and the sun, and how their dispute over how to share the weather was resolved," said her mum, pulling her on her knees before she started.

"Long ago", began, "the rain and the sun were good friends and shared the weather in harmony, until one of them became greedy and there was a dispute. When asked what was the cause of the dispute, the rain said that the sun took too much time to shine and stole the opportunity to rain, while the sun argued that the rain, as soon as it could, it didn't want to stop and it kept raining. The dispute continued until one day the rainbow got tired, came forward to solve the problem and said to them: "I will be the judge on this matter. Every time the rain falls heavily and its turn ends, I will appear in the sky so that you, Mr Sun, will know that it is your turn to shine, which means that I will be the one who decides when the rain stops and you shine. When you see Mr Dark Cloud, you will know that your turn is over, which means Dark Cloud will decide when you stop and the rain will start again, as Mr Cloud and I are impartial". Both accepted and since then, every time there is a heavy rain shower, in the end, the rainbow appears to signal the end of the rain".

"I wish the rainbow could appear now," said Suzie.

"In time, my dear, your rainbow will appear," said Mother, caressing her.

So the next day it stopped raining but Suzie refused to go out and play. She stood at the window watching her friends play.

"It stopped raining, Suzie, why don't you join your friends?" Mum asked her in surprise.

"I haven't seen the rainbow yet and so I know that the rain isn't over yet." she said, smiling at her mum. It didn't take long for the rain to come back and Suzie was happy not to have gone out.

The next day Suzie woke up and saw clearly the rainbow in the sky, ran to her mother and said: "Today the rainbow came out and now I can go out to play".

"Yes, dear, the rain is finally over," replied her mother as she watched her run out to join Thelma and Bobby, who were already waiting outside.

Summary:
Sometimes we have to be patient and wait for the right time. If Suzie hadn't been patient and gone out to play, the rain would have wet her and she would have been sad. Instead she was wise and waited for the rainbow to appear.

BRAVE ANNIE

Once upon a time, there was a girl named Annie Johnson. She lived with her parents in a big city in Texas. Mr. and Mrs. Johnson were both doctors at a large hospital in the city and always very busy at work. Most of the time, Annie spent the day, after school, alone or at Stacy's house, who was her best friend, waiting for them. Her parents used to pick her up from Stacy's after work. Annie and Stacy would often do homework, then watch TV or play hide-and-seek and go hide in the yard. Most of the time, Annie watched Stacy and the other kids ride their bikes up and down the street. The other kids often made fun of Annie because she didn't have a bike. She didn't know how to ride a bike, and she was afraid to get hurt, and that made Annie very sad.

One Saturday morning, Mrs. Johnson didn't go to work because she had a day off. She was in the kitchen making breakfast when Annie came in crying.

"Hey, honey, what's wrong?" Mrs. Johnson asked as she turned to Annie.

"I want a bike, Mom, my friends make fun of me because I don't have one".

"Oh honey, I'm so sorry!" her mother said as she hugged her.

"I'll get you a bike right after breakfast, okay?" said his mother with a smile.

"Really?" Annie said excitedly.

"Oh yes, honey, I hope it cheers you up," said his mother.

"Yes, Mom, thank you," Annie smiled.

After breakfast, Annie and her mother went to the mall to get the bike. Her mother gave her a pink bike: pink is Annie's favorite color.

"Thanks mom, I love the bike! Now I can ride with my friends."

"I'm glad you like it, honey," his mother answered as they drove home.

The next morning, Annie had finished her morning chores, so she went to Stacy's house with her bike. Stacy was already with Richard, Josh and the other kids: they were about to ride their bikes.

"Hey Stacy, wait for me!", she cried as she took the bike to the other children.

"Nice bike," Stacy said.

"Let's see if she can beat me in a race," Josh added with a nasty look. Annie ignored him.

She got on his bike and tried to leave, but she couldn't. Every time she tried to pedal, she fell from the bike.

"Look how she falls," Richard said laughing, and others joined.

"She can't even ride a simple bike!" Josh added.

"I'm sure she will the last!" added the other boy, while the rest of the children laughed while riding away.

"Don't worry, Annie, I'll teach you how to ride a bike," Stacy said and helped her get back on her feet. Annie nodded sadly as the two friends left the other children. Stacy spent the rest of the day teaching Annie how to ride a bike.

Later in the evening, Annie came home, parked her bike in the garage and entered the house. She saw her parents in the living room watching TV. She greeted them in a sad tone and went straight to his room.

"I wonder what's wrong with Annie," said Mr. Johnson.

"I think we should talk to her," said Mrs. Johnson.

"Definitely !" said Mr. Johnson as they went straight to Annie's room.

"Hey Annie, what's the matter, honey?" his father asked as he entered the room.

"I can't ride a bike," she said.

"Oh dear," her mother said as she sat beside her.

"Don't worry, Annie, I'll teach you how to ride a bike," her father said and caressed her cheek.

"But Dad, you and Mom are always busy at work, you barely have time for me..."

"Oh, honey, your father and I will make time for you," said her mother.

"Yes, we promise to always find time for you no matter what," her father added with a smile.

"Cheer up, honey, we promise, okay?" added her mother, smiling.

"All right," Annie said.

"You know, honey, with determination, practice, concentration and love I'm sure you'll learn to ride a bike," said Annie's dad and he kissed her on the cheek. Then they both hugged her.

The next day, after breakfast, Mr. and Mrs. Johnson took Annie out to teach her how to ride a bike.

"Hold on to your handlebars, honey, hold your chin up, pedal and just focus on the road," her father said as he held on to her bike and started pushing it.

"All right, Dad, but don't leave me," Annie said as she was riding on her bike, focused on the road.

"Trust me, honey, I got you, you just need to focus on the road and control the bike".

"Go, honey, I know you can, make Mom proud," Annie's mom cheered from behind as she watched.

Mr. Johnson pushed the bike with Annie and made her ride a few more feet before he let her go. She didn't realize her father had left his bike.

"Dad, don't ever leave me, I'll fall if you do," Annie said while she was still pedaling. She was so focused she didn't realize her father had left the bike almost two minutes ago.

"No, honey, you're already doing it".

Annie looked back and saw that her father was not holding her. She became enthusiastic and continued with determination.

"Yes!! I did it, I can ride a bike".

"Mom, look at me, I did it," said happy Annie.

"Yes, honey, I knew you could!" cried Annie's mom.

Then Annie turned to her parents, stopped the bike and gave them a big hug.

Summary:

If you want to achieve something in life, you must be determined, work hard towards your goal and always be focused. No great man has grown up without applying any of these tips.

Description

Are you looking for a children's book that can make Bedtime a wonderful time?

Are you looking to help your kids get away from technology and go back into a land that is based solely on their imagination?

These stories are both fun and will teach kids a wonderful lesson as they fall asleep. No matter which one you pick, though, you are sure to have a story that they will treasure.

The stories here are sure to transform children's bedtime experience, while also giving them plenty to think about, learn about, and grow with. This book was written for children of all ages, so as long as they still enjoy having a bedtime story read, they will adore this book!

Many people are habitual of reading bedtime stories to their children. It is usually considered to be a fun activity however; it can also play a key role in building the personality of a child. Moreover, parents get a chance to spend quality time with their children. This enables them to strengthen the family bond. Bedtime stories also help children in relaxing their minds. Thus, it helps them to have a sound and comfortable sleep. Apart from these, bedtime stories enhance the imagination of a child. It is because in these stories they encounter characters and scenes which they do not see commonly in their daily lives. Moreover, bedtime stories also play a major role in developing critical thinking and problem-solving skills of children. All these skills ensure better development of your kid's personality.

This book is written keeping in view all the above-mentioned factors. Various stories in the book will help you to mold the personality and thoughts of your child. It will be the right choice for you and your children. The stories in this book are fiction. Reading them to your children will foster the bond between you two. The values, morals, etc. that you will discuss with your child will help him to become a good person. It will enhance the interest and learning abilities of him. Thus, sharing bedtime stories with kids is something all the parents should make a part of their daily routine.

This book is a collection of perfect bedtime stories. Make them a part of your daily routine so that your child develops a habit of learning new things every day.

Find a comfy spot that's free of distractions, cuddle up with your kids, and enjoy these stories!

THE END

CPSIA information can be obtained
at www.ICGtesting.com
Printed in the USA
BVHW041530131120
593255BV00016B/1128

9 781801 116305